Grace and Forgiveness in Ministry

Murray Stewart Thompson

Abingdon
NASHVILLE

Grace and Forgiveness in Ministry

Library of Congress Cataloging in Publication Data

THOMPSON, MURRAY STEWART, 1923–
   Grace and forgiveness in ministry.
   Includes bibliographical references.
   1. Pastoral theology.   2. Pastoral counseling.   3. Thompson,
Murray Stewart, 1923– I. Title.
BV4011.T44   253.5   80-23613

ISBN 0-687-15680-7

Scripture quotations unless otherwise noted are from the
Revised Standard Version of the Bible, copyrighted 1946,
1952, © 1971, 1973 by the Division of Christian Education
of the National Council of the Churches of Christ in the
U.S.A.

MANUFACTURED BY THE PARTHENON PRESS AT
NASHVILLE, TENNESSEE, UNITED STATES OF AMERICA

Dedicated to
intrepid adventurers in life,
Margaret, David, Gregg, Paul,
Blair, and Susan

Contents

Preface

This is a personal document. In a sense this is true of any book ever authored. In this case the uniqueness rests in the frank acknowledgment or the daring claim that whatever is of value in it is likely to be seen in the interplay between person and context, between experience and concept, between past and present, present and future, in the lives of two people.

The subject is ministry, a concept with many facets, definitions, and meanings inherited from the past, currently operative in our midst, and struggling toward expression in the future. The personal life and experience is my own and that of a patient with whom I worked intensively for a period of seven months and with whom I have had occasional contact now for some sixteen years. The ongoing reflection is mine. The context, against the background of nearly two thousand years of Christian history, is the parish, the hospital, the counseling center, the home, and the wider community in which I have sought to enlarge my understanding of ministry and extend my ability to minister.

Because I am addressing a mixed audience, laypersons wishing to discover or extend a new area of ministry for them, clergy looking for new skills or a secure integration of belief and practice, theologians working to refine and sharpen the articulation of the "faith once delivered to the saints" for a fast-changing world, professional counselors, lay counselors, and students in training curious about whether inherited perspectives of God and man as spirit can contribute to their understanding and practice, I offer the following roadmap. If you are a professional pastor or theologian you will want to read chapter 1 first. If you are a Christian you may well want to begin in the same place. You may, on the other hand, wish to push on to the personal. Chapter 2 is an autobiographical sketch of my life up to the point of my year as a chaplain-intern in a program of Clinical Pastoral Education.

Chapters 3, 4, and 5 are heavily experiential. The central feature of these chapters is an intensive and extensive examination of my attempts to minister to one patient bearing the diagnosis "chronic schizophrenic, paranoid type." The data under study consists of extracts from some thirty-six sessions with this patient, whom we will call Mrs. Jones, over a seven-month period. The record is in the form of verbatim reports, essentially reconstructions from memory after each session of what was said and of the context including the nonverbal. Such reconstructions are a major tool for supervision in Clinical Pastoral Education. They are submitted with analysis and evaluation to the supervisor and are the basis for individual supervision and peer-group review. Though filtered by the conscious and unconscious processes of the student, verbatims have proven to be a reliable way of identifying the characteristic personal responses of the would-be minister in relation to the person in need. To my reflection and evaluation of that time I have added, verbatim by verbatim, the longitudinal view from this point in time including present judgments and with some knowledge of subsequent events in the life of Mrs. Jones.

The division between chapters 3, 4, and 5 is unequal and somewhat arbitrary. They put into words what puzzled me greatly at the time and continued to intrigue me long after the active relationship had ceased. That there was something of very real significance in the relationship throughout seemed self-evident. Why, however, was there a period of approxi-mately three months when the patient appeared to be making marked progress toward health? Why for approximately two months did her condition, outwardly at least, deteriorate almost to the level of her earlier condition? Why was there another change of direction which led two months later to discharge after five years of almost continuous hospitalization? Each chapter looks at one of these phases.

Subsequent to my work with Mrs. Jones I enrolled in a seminary course dealing with the Letter of Paul to the Romans. It was in seminar format, and I elected to do a paper on the concept of righteousness. When I had lived with that subject for a while I was struck with the parallels between the biblical concept and my experiences with Mrs. Jones. For my Master's thesis I examined both closely under the title "The Relevance of the Doctrine of Justification by Faith for Pastoral Care—An Idiographic Study." A precis of that thesis is the substance of chapter 6.

The significance of this relationship for the patient may possibly be exaggerated. The epilogue will give some details of her subsequent history and something of her evaluation of the relationship from the perspectives of ten years and then sixteen years. Her life is not an exhibit in support of claims to messianic fulfillment. Yet her life is different, and she is grateful. Though there can be no proof concerning the cause of the changes in her, it seems plausible to look closely at our relationship to see what may have been operative for her good. As for me that experience has resulted in a radical aboutface, a new awakening to the dynamics of ministry, and led to a new appreciation of the heritage of faith to which I seek to be a witness. Chapter 7 seeks to convey my present stage in a personal quest to be a minister as a professional in the church, a believer among believers, and a human being with needs, willing to give to and to receive from other human beings as opportunity may afford.

In writing so personally I feel the more heavily responsibility for acknowledgments. There is the community which nurtured me, my parents in particular, also the teachers, the Sunday school teachers, the various church fellowships which through the years have symbolized and exercised judgment and acceptance and hope. My professors and colleagues have done the same over many years: the staff of the Institute of Religion in Houston, Texas, during those years of training, notably Dawson Bryan, Joseph Knowles, Leroy Kerney, Edward Thornton, and Tom Cole, the late Dr. Jack Simons, ward physician of the Veterans Hospital and Becky Smith, head nurse, should be included. The staff of the Pastoral Institute of British Columbia, Tom Bulman, Barry Cooke, Vince D'Monte, Betty Atkinson, and its board of directors, warrant special mention.

Mrs. Jones, my collaborator from the outset who welcomed me as a "man of the cloth" and as a learner in Clinical Pastoral Education, has continued to offer her friendship and collaboration, and indeed, her encouragement to me. Otherwise I would not be offering this book.

Three persons have assisted me in the preparation of the text, Therese D'Monte with her typing and gracious encouragement, her husband, Vince, who assisted with punctuation, and Kay Francis who typed the revisions.

There is another group who have ministered unto me and upon whom I have depended grealty to keep me alive and growing. I refer to my wife, Margaret, with whom I have shared the daily challenge of seeking togetherness in the face of differences. Without her cooperation, courage, and willingness to sacrifice I would not have been in Texas. Without her patience, her perseverance, and her loyalty I would have been deprived of the security so necessary to my functioning. Her willingness to give and to take, her courage to be herself, has provided me with a continuous opportunity to minister and to be ministered unto. She with our family of four sons and a daughter know me as no others do at those points where I feel most under judgment and each has a unique way of letting me know that they care.

I

The Who and the How of Ministry

When I started my search for answers to questions arising from my work with Mrs. Jones, I nurtured the hope that what I discovered might be of some significance to the field of counseling and psychotherapy. I still hold out that hope and offer what follows with that in mind. I felt at the time, and now know, that there is very little counseling skill in the data I present. The learning for some may be in identifying what not to do! I was offering what I could at that time and something positive happened. That led me to conclude that my experience could be useful to the large number of people who know they lack professional skills yet who would like to be and believe they can be more helpful than they now perceive themselves to be. I began to think not only of pastors lacking special training in pastoral skills but also of laypersons who aspire to be more creative in relation to family, friends, neighbors, or anyone else who is experiencing stress of one kind or another. I was also mindful of the gulf which has existed, and in large measure continues to exist, between pastoral counselors and specialists in pastoral care on the one hand, and theologians and traditional clergy on the other. To the latter the new breed of clergy are suspect, practitioners of an alien art derived from psychology. To the former, the theologian tends to live in another world and the traditional pastor is mired in the sands of antiquity.

Many years have lapsed since my attention first came into focus concerning the nature of a helping or therapeutic relationship. I continue to live with the same issues as they appear in new forms in the course of my life as a professional minister. I have concluded that the root question for me is: What is the nature of ministry? What does it mean to minister to another person? What is involved in being a minister?

Those questions have been around for a long time. They were a major issue at the time of the Reformation. From that time until now there have been waves of anti-clericalism. The roots of that spirit are many and varied. Sometimes it grows from the experienced disparity between what the ministry purports to be and what it actually is. Sometimes it seems to stem from resistance to the claims to authority which have no adequate basis in Scripture. Sometimes it represents a vague but persistent protest against incompetence.

There has always been a ministry in the church, for the Christian call is a call to service. For that service God has provided a variety of gifts: "And his gifts were that some should be apostles, some prophets, some evangelists, some pastors and teachers, to equip the saints for the work of ministry, for building up of the body of Christ" (Eph. 4:11-12). As Thomas Mullen has said, "It is always bad to make religion professional. It is not bad to make the pastor a professional."[1]

The Reformation attacked the former at its roots by reaffirming the priesthood of all believers. By this doctrine it proclaimed belief in the ability, the privilege, and the responsibility of each individual to worship God directly and personally. No intermediary is required or possible. By implication the essential distinction between clergy and the faithful, as it had been understood, was erased. There is, the Reformers declared, an essential equality though the clergy and the laity fulfill somewhat different functions.

The same tension that was present at the time of the Reformation reappeared in the protests of the Quakers in the seventeenth century. They cried out against the privileges, the honors, and the status accorded to the clergy solely because they were clergy. Their objections were not to clergy functions but to the unwarranted claims to recognition and power associated with the office. It has been said that the Quakers did not reject a professional ministry. Rather, they had no laypersons, no differential in status, only acknowledgment of individual functions and gifts.

American church history is replete with examples of the same struggle. Few Christian movements have avoided a fulltime ministry. It seems to be inevitable and generally is accepted as having scriptural justification. The largest home-grown denomination, the Disciples of Christ, has traveled that road.

More recently there have been many stirrings among the laity concerning their ministry. These have been in many forms. In the Roman Catholic church, especially since Vatican II, the lay apostolate has been taken much more seriously. The Oxford Movement of the 1930s and the Faith-at-Work movement have both stressed the ministry of the laity. The charismatic movement, which has blossomed across many denominational lines has had this same quality of affirming the ministry of all believers. Not long ago I sat in on a gathering of Unitarians and found that they were discussing a conference where the place of the professional ministry was a topic of major interest.

The denominations rest more or less uneasily with the current ferment within the arenas of the local parish and the larger jurisdictions. Traditional attitudes and practices do not give way without tension and conflict. For every parishioner who seeks or demands change there is another who requires the status quo. For every minister or priest who is seeking to redefine his role or to implement a new one there is another who anxiously defines the model for which he was trained.

The consequences for the life of the church are hard to assess. Many churches in North America in the 1980s are having a hard time. That judgment assumes the traditional criteria, statistics regarding attendance, professions of faith,

Sunday school attendance, givings adjusted for inflation and for the general standard of living, biblical literacy, and moral influence. Despite some evidence of vitality here and there, especially among some of the more conservative evangelical and fundamentalist churches, the drift away from the churches is pronounced. Does this represent a denial of the faith or a rejection of its institutional forms? Does it mean rejection of doctrine or flight from the necessity of contending with other believers whose conceptions of the church are either more radical or more conservative than their own? Are they tired of being exploited or disillusioned through long years of undernourishment and underemployment? Is the concept of ministry at the heart of the problem?

A longtime student of the church and of the ministry is Seward Hiltner. Much of his energy over the years has focused on the functions of ministry, the role of the professional minister, and the training of the clergy. In this respect he has been in the vanguard of the church's thinking. He has been its critic and also a patient and persistent agent working for change. Yet in *Ferment in the Ministry* he makes what I would call a spirited defense against the popular criticisms of the church and its impact, past and present.[2] His book is a response to the air of crisis in the professional ministry, of which there have been and are so many signs. Like Mullen and numerous others, he takes seriously the breakdown of many ministers, the crises in their families, the exodus from the ministry, the flight from the pastorate, the decline (now reversed) in seminary enrollment, the quality of candidates presenting themselves for vocations in the church. In doing so he nonetheless affirms the validity of the professional ministry. He attempts with real success, I think, to provide a balanced conceptual framework derived from his extensive knowledge of history and of the contemporary world scene.

Denominations, too, wrestle with the task of devising appropriate structures for expressing the ministry of the whole church. My own denomination, the United Church of

Canada, over a period of years has invested considerable money, time, and effort in defining the nature of ministry in the twentieth century. This undertaking was inspired, in part, by union negotiations with the Anglican Church in Canada which had reached a critical stage. Perhaps that is why its earliest efforts were judged incomplete. While professing to believe that there is only one ministry of God, his ministry to the world through the whole people of God, the commission's report concerned itself largely with the "ordered" ministry, the clergy and other fulltime servants of the church. Some of its recommendations were implemented at once, intended to alleviate some of the confusion, stress, and distress of its professionals. The General Council received the report with its definition of the Order of Ministry (known as the "Ministry of Word and Sacraments") having three functions: oversight, pertaining to the ministries and structures of the church; pastoral, pertaining to life in and service to the fellowship; and service, pertaining to service in and to the world. It accepted the view that these functions are not hierarchical in relation to each other but lateral. Then it directed a new task force "to set the report in the context of an adequate statement concerning the ministry of Christ as entrusted to the whole people of God."[3] I will attempt to highlight the main thrust of the response to that directive.

First, ministry starts with God, the One who declares himself in the history of Israel and in Jesus Christ as the Creator of all things. Christians believe that God has a purpose for creation and that he will see it through.

Second, though we cannot know the fullness of God's intention for the world or for the human race, we can see evidence of him in nature, in history, in the hearts of his servants, but above all through Jesus, the Word made flesh, and through the continuing activity of the Holy Spirit speaking and moving though persons in our own day. That he has acted to bring humanity into a living fellowship with himself and with one another, and, indeed, with the whole created order is the conviction underlying the whole of Scripture.

15

Third, Christians believe that this at-one-ment happens through the presence and action of God in Jesus Christ. However it may be explained, sin, or alienation, is real, and we are in any ultimate sense impotent in the face of it. Without the gospel, the good news of God's saving action, the exhortation to do justly and love mercy, and like admonitions, to follow the Golden Rule, to love the brethren, and to take up one's cross are simply bad news. The Christian life then, is the life lived in response to the good news. Normally it is lived in the context of the church. There is the recognition that there is universal judgment and a like need for regeneration but that it is presumptuous of any person or church to make judgments concerning those outside the church.

The call to ministry may well be experienced by anyone inside the church or outside it, for there are many whose objectives coincide with the at-one-ment of all creation, and God seems to bless their efforts. In the context of the church, though, ministry is to be understood as having two ingredients: the call of God and the human response. This call is the same for everyone. Jesus' call to all people is "Follow me." Yet within that inclusive call there are specific or personal calls to particular tasks or responsibilities. Without denigrating the worthwhileness of unconscious acts of service, Christian ministry is to be understsood as a conscious response to the call of God. Hence the excitement and the vitality experienced by members of the laity when they first realize that what they may have been doing at home or at work is a ministry in the same sense as that of the clergy.

The theological foundation for ministry is summarized thus:

We believe this: That we are in the hands of God who is active in His creation, wrestling with it in its perversities and its glories. We believe that His nurturing, redemptive love has acted in history with power and victory in the person of Christ, that we are called to respond to that gift and participate in His wrestling with Creation. We know that we are not alone but that God's spirit equips us and empowers us through a variety of gifts which we are called to use in His service. The basic thrust of that call we believe to be unchanging and common to us all; because God is active in history then we believe that the specifics of that call, however mediated, will be different for particular individuals and will change even for those individuals as the created order groans toward its fulfillment. Our response will also vary. The task of the Church is to provide structures so that the intent of God's call and the objectives of its specific manifestations may be actualized in the world.[4]

What the report identifies as common to all forms of ministry are two things, witness and being. It is not our work or our words but Jesus Christ who ministers. We do what we can to open doors and to make connections. Ministry involves authentic living, being. There can be no avoidance of the question "What kind of person are you because the gospel has touched your life?" Messenger and message must be congruent. A life that believes in people and enjoys the companionship of others speaks. It emerges from a self-awareness, a self-acceptance, and a self-identity rooted in a sure knowledge of the faith, which makes possible the exercise of stewardship over all one's gifts for ministry. It permits one the ability to say yes and to say no while fully conscious and committed to responsibility for the neighbor. That responsibility is both personal and corporate. Hence part of our ministry is through participation in the programs of the church and through the institutions and structures that make up our world.

As I reflect on such a comprehensive view of ministry in which the laity share fully with the clergy, I see a plethora of possibilities, opportunities, and expectations which seem all but overwhelming. By what handles can a layperson grapple with the church in the world? Is the predicament of the clergy any different?

No church is facing questions related to ministry with greater earnestness than the Catholic church. Few can imagine the prodigious labors which must have gone into the preparation for Vatican II. Since then the energies employed have multiplied almost beyond belief. Not all have had the blessings of the Holy Father and some efforts, more than others, have been the occasion for increased confusion and apprehension. Recently, as I scanned the shelves of the University of Winnipeg under the heading of ministry I was drawn to four titles: *Ministry in the Church* by Andre Lemaire,[5] *Why Priests?* by Hans Kung,[6] and two volumes by Henri J. Nouwen, *The Wounded Healer*[7] and *Creative Ministry.*[8] All are Catholic authors and all are part of the continuing dialogue.

I know of no better brief statement concerning the New Testament basis for ministry and its historic evolution in the church than that of Lemaire. The book cover refers to him as "a French Roman Catholic priest who studied theology in Paris under Oscar Cullman." For a straightforward but I think not a simplistic treatment of the subject, I refer you to his book. I will outline those aspects of his discussion which seem pertinent to my purpose.

Jesus gathered many disciples and from these he chose twelve. They were known as The Twelve, not apostles. We don't know much about the special instruction he gave them or how it was accomplished. We do know that he gave them a mandate: "Truly, I say to you, in the new world, when the Son of man shall sit on his glorious throne, you who have followed me will also sit on twelve thrones, judging the twelve tribes of Israel" (Matt. 19:28; Luke 22:28-30). Lemaire understands the judging function in the Old Testament sense of leading, deciding, commanding, exercising the power of a ruler. The impact of Jesus' teaching and example, however, was such as to overthrow or reinterpret all their inherited ideas concerning the exercise of such power.

When The Twelve lost one of their number they quickly invoked God's aid in choosing a replacement. Moreover, when the realities of their life required it they did not hesitate with God's guidance and in consultation with all the people to create a new ministerial framework. The qualifications for office were not unlike their own. They chose seven men from among the Hellenists.

The Seven had a very brief history so far as it is known to us. Stephen was killed, and we hear no more of them. The same is true of The Twelve. When James was killed we hear nothing of a replacement. A new kind of minister appeared. Missionary work led to the choice of apostles, a word meaning "one who is sent." Saul (Paul) and Barnabas were the first of this new breed. Paul became the leading apostle to the Gentiles and Peter of the Hebrew Christian community. Very soon the ministry of the church was recorded as including apostles, prophets, and teachers. Apostles were, first and foremost, missionaries. Prophets were primarily leaders in worship and entrusted with the proclamation of the Word through oracles, preaching, and leadership in prayers, notably of thanksgiving. Teachers were responsible for more systematic instruction, though the close relationship of the functions of prophet and teacher have been well established. Though this pattern of organization was common, it appears not to have been uniform throughout the church.

There are references to elders in the Jerusalem church and in others having an essentially Hebrew background. The term referred to the leadership or oversight function common to the Jewish community. In other congregations of the Greek mission, the common reference for the same function is to bishops and ministers, there being no indications of any hierarchy to the end of New Testament times. Whatever the title of such officeholders, the concern was for unity and for fidelity to the teachings of Jesus and the teaching concerning him.

Lemaire says that Jesus provided the ministry for his church and that Paul, like his Master, recognized the importance of order and provided for it in place of anarchy and disorder. Paul used the figures of body and building to convey his concern. For him there was no incongruity between institution and charismatic gift. Both were of the Spirit. Luke and John who made much of the Holy Spirit also associated the Spirit with the order that was given. Persons with gifts in the church were not merely a derivative of the body but a gift to the body from its Head. They were his representatives.

The uniqueness of the authority vested in Jesus' ministers is in the manner in which that authority is exercised. The most appropriate words to describe it are servant, steward, slave, the very opposite of the raw power commonly exercised by rulers, and the primary association of that authority was with the proclamation of the Word. It was not, in Lemaire's words, "above the people but for the people, as one of them." Moreover, while there was a specific responsibility resting upon those thus designated it was not an exclusive thing. " 'Teacher, we saw a man casting out demons in your name, and we forbade him, because he was not following us.' But Jesus said, 'Do not forbid him; for no one who does a mighty work in my name will be able soon after to speak against me' " (Mark 9:38-39). Paul exercised his authority in much the same fashion. Even when he spoke with the greatest force there was an implicit, if not an explicit, appeal for their best judgment so that their compliance, which he very much desired, might be, as it were, a mutual decision. Other references could be cited which suggest limits to personal power, specifically limits stemming from the unmistakable gifts bestowed upon others in the community of faith.

Turning now to Hans Kung, the renowned if controversial Catholic theologian, we find the same point being made. He summarizes his discussion of leadership in the church by identifying four characteristics of it: "It must (a) be a service to the congregation; (b) follow Jesus' norm, which permits no relationship of domination; (c) remain bound to the primary apostolic testimony; (d) exist in the midst of a plurality of different functions, ministries, charisms."[9]

Kung takes issue with the direction which the early church took under pressure from political, social, and pagan sources. In particular, he attempts an explanation for the historic controversy among the churches over valid orders. He finds nothing by way of scriptural authority for the Catholic church's adherence to a sacramentalism which incorporates the idea of a repeated sacrifice on the altar. Therefore he finds no basis for a priesthood possessing the powers necessary to transform the elements into the actual body and blood of Christ. He rejects the status, privilege, and authority derived from the possession of such power. Discussing the appropriate qualities for leadership in the church he says:

Function and position in the Church, much less the power and public prestige which may accompany these cannot be of ultimate importance for the church leader. The members of any group, ecclesiastical or not, are always vitally interested in the following, without which leadership cannot function and a credibility gap arises at once: Does the person at the top really believe what he is saying? Is he convinced that the road to which he points is the right one? Does he regard the goal he proposes as attainable? Does he believe? For the leader of a Christian community this last question is fundamental in a very special way. Belief here means that the believer commits self with absolute confidence to the Christian message with all the theoretical and practical consequences than ensue for self, that he thus commits himself and his whole existence to Jesus and His cause.[10]

And again: "What is really important is whether and to what extent he is purely and simply a believer; that is, to what extent he, together with all others in this community of free people with equal rights, of brothers and sisters, is one who believes, loves and hopes."[11]

The common denominator for lay Christian and for professional minister alike is a living and personal witness to the faith by whatever gifts and opportunities seem appropriate to the occasion. Both encounter resistance to change. Religion has had its long tradition of inducing and sustaining change and growth, medicine the same. With the ascendancy of rational and empirical methods of science, both have come to rely more and more on methods working with the consciousness of the individual, to the neglect of the unconscious. In the case of psychotherapy and counseling, in particular, the objectives of therapy were seen to be served through making the unconscious part of the conscious, assuming that in consciousness is the power to make appropriate change. The results have been disappointing. The resistance to understanding is great. The resistance to change is greater. Therapists like Milton Erickson in psychiatry and Jay Haley in family therapy are now stressing the necessity of accepting the resistance and of trying to incorporate it in a strategy of action which pushes the individual or the family into new situations and forces an untried solution to a problem in living. The demands of the live situation harness both the conscious and the unconscious processes and seem to be more effective in producing change, especially where resistance to new patterns of behaving has been pronounced.

The traditional methods of the Christian church have been increasingly less effective with large numbers of people. That may well be one of the unconscious elements in the atmosphere of crisis in the church. The conscious panic may be in response to the change which the church experiences in the response of her people and of the world. Underneath may be the vague awareness that all is not well with the church's life and that the church itself is like the sinner and the patient, professing the desire for health and/or salvation but resistive to conscious prescription or direction. The symptom appears as a crisis in leadership. The treatment equal to the need is a strategy which takes seriously the resistance and breaks new ground while holding to the verities of the gospel.

From this view the need is that of the whole people of God and the strategy must include the whole people of God. The relationship between the layperson and the professional may well be of crucial importance. Henri J. Nouwen in his book *Creative Ministry* pushes consistently for the necessity of getting beyond professionalism. His book is addressed to the functions of apostolic ministry which he identifies as missionary outreach, preaching, teaching, caring, organizing, and celebrating. Whatever the function, he concludes that it must be grounded in the spiritual life of the practitioner. That is at one and the same time highly personal and also very catholic. Because it is so catholic he says:

It will become clear that every Christian is a minister. The ordained minister can be considered a focus since the ordained minister gives the most visible shape to the different forms of Christian service. But what is true for ministers and priests in the formal sense is true for every man and woman who wants to live his life in the light of the Gospel of Jesus Christ. Therefore, in essence, this book is about the life-style of every Christian.[12]

The inner life of the believer has a common ground, and the outer world of laity and clergy alike presents the same need and the same resistance to health and salvation, for need implies change. Nouwen deals with the challenge of teaching against just such a background. We expect our clergy to be educated, to go to university and seminary in the interests of a fuller grasp of the Gospel and of the world to which it is addressed. The common assumption is that before this experience the candidate lacks knowledge, and that given the knowledge, the deficit will be overcome. The fact seems to be that many are poorly motivated to absorb more than a fraction of what knowledge and understanding is made available to them. Many more have great difficulty in using what they have acquired at the conscious level. So great is the resistance to the process of change. As teachers in their turn, they face the same problem in trying to pass on to others what seems to be so important to them. How does one motivate those who seem so little interested in learning? What can one do about those multitudes who know what they can and should do, but do not translate their knowledge into action?

Much of our educational methodology fails to take such ambivalence toward learning into account. It tends to assume desire and to ignore or merely lament the other. The result commonly is a preoccupation with content and neglect of the person whose energies must be enlisted if creative learning is to take place. The resistance to learning is associated with the sense of irrelevance. Underneath that half-conscious judgment are feelings related to the possible personal consequences of new knowledge. It is not a rational assessment but an emotional response which precludes serious commitment. Yet our educational system at every level is heavily invested in the rational and the conceptual realms, and despite some movement in that direction, not really convinced that the emotional and the personal are a legitimate concern of the educator. It is sometimes recognized in the provision of counseling services, much more rarely in the standard preparation of those who teach.

The implications are of critical importance for the church. If the methods of the seminary are essentially rational and conceptual, the same emphasis is likely to be dominant among parish clergy and in their efforts to teach. How likely is it that the church school and its teacher or the confirmation class will be any different? While teaching and preaching have always been associated in some degree, the intent of preaching has commonly been understood as going beyond the imparting of knowledge. It has been more overtly interested in the influencing of behavior. Some of the best preachers I know are good teachers. They convey a wealth of information in a way which makes it seem to be important. It is no effort to listen. But with the information there is another impact. The heart is touched as well as the mind and so is the impulse to action. Preaching is an appeal to the will. The appeal is not to the irrational but to that which goes beyond reason. One might say that the address is to the whole person.

The problem of the preacher is not unlike that of the teacher. Why is it that sermons are not more appreciated? Why is it that they are not more effective in shaping the lives of people? What is the secret of the power exercised by a few? How does one learn to be an effective preacher? It is assumed, but is it right to assume, that one goes to seminary to learn this art? Are the chief ingredients knowledge of the subject, namely, the Gospel, and the structure and style of delivery?

How important is knowledge of the life experience of the people addressed? Is the critical factor the self-awareness of the preacher and the extent to which the preacher is able and willing to show the relationship between his experience of the faith and the events of his own life?

Certainly, a personal witness can be a powerful influence, and that of the pulpit ought not to be denied. The minister, pastor, or priest has always been aware of the opportunities and responsibilities in his personal dealings with the people of parish and community. It is more so now. Pastoral care and counseling are seen as traditional functions. Yet recent decades have seen the emergence of a special interest, a special literature, a specialist function, and a network of training centers devoted to the caring ministry. What is vital in a truly helpful change- and growth-inducing relationship? What produces results of the desired order? Is it knowledge and skills derived from psychology and the social sciences? Is there anything uniquely effective about Christian caring? If so, what? Clinical Pastoral Education (CPE), including pastoral counseling, has been sought by thousands of clergy and theological students. The popular perception of many who come and of those who disdain to come is that they will gain knowledge, techniques, and skills which they may then apply in pastoral work. The surprise, for many, is that the process does not stop with knowledge, techniques, and skills. The focus narrows inevitably to the examination of the uniqueness of the person who would reach out the helping hand to another who is also unique. The would-be minister is confronted with the nature of the ultimate gift, not a directive, not a doctrine or a concept but a person, a struggling, seeking, growing, believing, yet humble servant of Jesus Christ, through whom he may become real.

It is my contention, as that of a growing number of others seems to be, that the secret of successful teaching, preaching, counseling, caring, organizing, celebrating by professional and nonprofessional alike, is to be found in the realm of the personal. The would-be minister must take seriously Paul's appeal:

I beseech you therefore, brethren, by the mercies of God, that ye present your bodies, a living sacrifice, holy, acceptable to God, which is your reasonable service. And be not conformed to this world, but be ye transformed by the renewing of your mind, that ye may prove what is that good, and acceptable, and perfect, will of God. For I say, through the grace given unto me, to every man that is among you, not to think of himself more highly than he ought to think; but to think soberly, according as God hath dealt to every man the measure of faith. (Rom. 12:1-3 KJV)

The ministry of writing is not one mentioned in the New Testament but such it has become. It, too, can be the vehicle of the personal, a means to convey the faith as it resides within. I have never been convinced that I have the gift of written communication, but I would like to have it. I do believe that I have something to share and that my sharing will be on two levels, the conscious and the unconscious. It is my growing experience that when I offer myself freely and gladly to another God can use me just as I am.

II

On Being Personal

May the 11th, 1923 may seem like any other date in history to others but not to me. That was my birthday. The light of day came to me in the little company hospital of an eastern Ontario mining village. The mine and the hospital have long since closed, but their reputation lives on, in part because of the tender loving care accorded my mother who waited week by week beyond the time when she had expected the arrival of her first-born.

I was given the name Murray Stewart Thompson, Murray because my parents liked it, Stewart because that was my mother's maiden name. Stewart sounded Scottish and many a Scot has been ready to acknowledge kinship. In fact, however, my Scottish relatives were far removed. On both sides of the house there was close to a century of eastern Ontario Canadian history and a mingling of English, Scottish, and Irish blood, the latter being predominant.

On my mother's side her great-grandfather had reputedly been the first physician in Bytown which was later to be called Ottawa. Some of his descendants took up farming in a new community to the west called Fort Stewart. There was timber to be cut, but the land was stony and none too productive. Fort Stewart remained a backwoods. My mother and her sister both left home while still in their early teens in order to attend high school. They went a hundred miles or so to Stirling where maternal relatives still lived. Later they were both to teach school.

Stirling was where she met my father. He was the second of three sons. His father was a cheese-maker turned farmer, both traditions common among his relatives. His older brother decided to stay with the farm. His younger brother entered the field of banking. But Robert Garner, my father, under the influence of the Methodist church which the family attended regularly, struck out for university with a view to entering the ministry. Though he was later to be known as a quiet, gentle person his inclinations found expression in several directions. In addition to his church there was music to engage him, specifically the glee club. There was also the debating society and a literary society which at one point awarded him a prize.

By this time the First World War was in progress. The university recruited and trained contingents of officers. My father went overseas in 1915 and was attached as a young officer to the Royal Warwickshire Regiment of the British Army. Before long he was in France. His unit took part in a number of important engagements but also saw long months of inaction. What seems to have come out of these experiences was the intensely felt conviction: "There must be a better way."

Whether through love of adventure, valor, or boredom, my father in 1917 transferred to the infant Royal Air Force. While training as an observer, he was injured in a plane crash. He walked with a slight limp for the rest of his life. A bone from his ankle, a service revolver, a helmet, binoculars, and a uniform are all part of my childhood memories. My brother and I played at being soldiers.

My father and mother became engaged by correspondence when Father was overseas. He was still intending to study theology so the wedding did not take place until 1920 on the eve of departure for a year's study in Edinburgh, Scotland. Ordination followed in 1921. From 1921 to 1925 my father served two pastorates in succession, less than thirty miles apart and scarcely more than that from the community in which he had been raised. I have only shadowy memories of the time after birth when we still lived close to grandparents. A vague recollection lingers of playing beneath a sewing machine, working the treadle, and feeling cozy and secure in the confined space with interested and kindly faces looking in on me.

The year 1925 was a historic one for the Methodist church in which I had been baptized and of which my father was a minister. It entered into union with the Presbyterian Church and the Congregational churches to form the United Church of Canada. For we Thompsons it meant a big move from old Ontario out west to Manitoba. There was a surplus of ministers in the east and my father was young and conscientious, ready to serve where needed. (My parents had applied for service in China but were turned down because of family health history.) Besides, my mother's family had previously abandoned the stony farmland of Fort Stewart with the bright promise of farming in Saskatchewan. The family was settled in a three-point rural charge a short distance from Portage-la-Prairie, Manitoba.

My memories increase of those years. A baby was added to the family. "Got two boys now, Mama" I used to say as I abandoned my bed after father got up to stoke up the coal and wood fires. My, how cold the house was, and how cozy to snuggle next to mother and my baby brother in her big bed!

There was singing. My parents both learned to play the piano as adults and my father continued to work at his playing through the years. He was more methodical than musical at the piano, less musical than my mother. But so far as my memory goes, they were both accomplished musicians and they liked to sing with us. "Here comes the pony, his work is all done . . ."

There was the sad day when my brother was seriously scalded. It was bath night. The water was being prepared: hot water from the top of the kitchen stove was in the round tub on the kitchen floor; father was pumping cold water from the cistern to cool it down; my brother and I were playing underfoot. Somehow my brother fell into the small tub. One hip and leg were affected. It meant a stay in the hospital in Portage-la-Prairie and a private room for a while with a big hoop over his bed to keep the weight of the blankets off the sensitive limb.

I don't remember being fitted for glasses. That happened during my fourth year. Apparently, it became obvious that there was an astigmatism which would not correct itself and, further, the vision in one eye was seriously deficient. I don't remember being fitted for the glasses but I do remember the stern warnings. I must be careful. If I engaged in strenuous activity which might be a threat, I was to take my glasses off. I remember one long anxious search because, in obedience, I had taken my glasses off to play soccer and had hidden them carefully in the long grass, but then couldn't recall just where I had placed them.

Oh, the minor distresses that parents have to endure! I'm sure it was a joke, not without its pain, when I discovered that it was much more fun to work with the lady next door than to do the same thing at home! I learned to ice-skate before I started school. In the process I received a gash over my right eye to the consternation of my parents who appreciated more than I did the threat to my eyesight.

School days started for me in Foxwarren, some two hundred miles from our first home in Manitoba. I remember the adventure of the trip to our new residence. The year was 1929 and highways were inching their way across the endless miles of prairie farmland. There were gravel roads and detours, rocks and mounds of earth, bumps and dust, teams of horses and scoops trailing behind them, men with sinewy arms and moisture laden tawny faces, and cars plunging and groaning their way through unknown perils.

The school building seemed big. Actually, there were seven rooms, two grades to a room except for the high school. It was a consolidated school district so many children came by van, car, or truck in the summer, horse-drawn sleigh in the winter. I lived on the other side of the village from the school. Whatever the distance, I think it was three-quarters of a mile, it seemed a long, long way. In winter there was an icy north wind. In summer my route took me through the center of the village where youths, some not so youthful, seemed to delight in teasing the "preacher's kid." As for the homeward journey, there were tempting side trips to visit the homes of friends. I remember no more sure way of rousing displeasure of my parents than failing to come home from school on schedule.

There were crises of other kinds. With a group of others I was summoned before the school principal. In grade 1 we had become intrigued with matches and had set fire to some dead grass. My brother, two years younger, not keen about school anyway, caught his thumb in the wringer of our new electric washing machine (electric power had just come to the village) soon after starting grade 1 and missed so much time because of that injury that he was withdrawn from school for the balance of the year. There was illness. I had enough colds and sore throats that medical opinion was that my tonsils should be removed. It was common practice to perform such a feat right at home. The doctor, who lived fourteen miles away, in the dead of winter came by horse and sleigh to our village. Using our kitchen as an operating theater, he administered the anesthetic only to discover that a vital instrument was miles beyond his reach. I came to, asking to see my tonsils, only to find that they remained undisturbed. A few weeks later another doctor performed the required operation but whooping cough and bronchial congestion intensified the anxieties of the winter.

My mother underwent major surgery during those years. I don't remember much about that. She was away in Winnipeg for a considerable length of time. I stayed with a chum on a farm where I had been a frequent visitor. It was an enjoyable time for me. Only later did I get some confused picture of the combination of urology and gynecology which resulted in "five operations in one." My mother's health for many years left much to be desired.

Her health did not prevent the adoption of a sister for her

two boys. There had been two miscarriages about which I knew nothing. Subsequently I learned that both would have been boys. There is a strong male tendency among Thompson heirs. My parents wanted a daughter and my brother and I a sister. It was much discussed amongst us. We boys were both brown-eyed with dark brown hair. We agreed we would like a fair-haired, blue-eyed baby. After the practice of the time, we actually visited a church home for unwed mothers. Yes, we knew about that. We saw several babies who were eligible for adoption. We quickly agreed on the one we wanted. She was neither fair-haired nor blue-eyed. She had sparkling brown eyes and brown hair. She was like us. We welcomed her into our house and home. The years from 1929 to 1934 were eventful in other ways and stressful too, though the stress was largely unnoticed by me. The house was old. The floor sloped so that marbles always collected at one side of each room. The floors were cold.

The world-wide depression and accompanying drought took its toll. I saw large numbers of hoboes riding the rods on freight trains. Though our house was far removed from the railway tracks, a considerable number of these unfortunate men found their way to the preacher's door asking for a meal or handout. I experienced some embarrassment one day when my younger brother engaged a man waiting to be served with food with the question "Are you a bum?"

Everyone experienced poverty, and the church responded in numerous ways. I recall boxcar loads of apples arriving from Ontario for distribution amongst our community. I also remember our community gathering and shipping boxcar loads of vegetables to be distributed amongst drought-stricken people in nearby Saskatchewan.

Few people had ready cash. Church finances were very difficult. The minister received some cash but much of his income was in kind: vegetables, fresh and frozen meat, butter, sour cream for churning, eggs, cracked wheat for porridge, and similar produce. Much of our clothing came from relatives, mine from a cousin who, because he was a little older and bigger and had parents who had more cash, conveniently outgrew his pants and suits and passed them on to me.

When I started to go to school I was trusted with a weekly allowance of ten cents. A designated portion was to be used for Sunday school offering, the rest was mine. That was 1929. The amount was soon reduced to a penny. This major experience with handling money was augmented from time to time by trapping gophers in the spring for which there was a small bounty. It was also a satisfaction on running an errand for the village butcher to be rewarded with a weiner for my personal consumption. Besides my farm chum, I had a village friend a little older than myself. The son of an English immigrant, he introduced me to his world of fantasy filled with ships. He could give the names of countless vessels large and small and hold me spellbound with accounts of disasters which had overtaken many. I became convinced that the safest way to travel to Europe would be by way of the Bering Strait!

We shared many things together, whether it was swinging hand over hand on the rafters of the livery barn adjacent to the church or exploring the hidden recesses under every bridge and culvert in the village. We made our first efforts to unravel some of the mysteries surrounding sex. We experimented with smoking of dry leaves and occasionally a tailor-made cigarette. Many hours were whiled away playing softball or variations thereof. Occasionally my father would take us hiking. Berry-picking in the summer was like a picnic.

Ministers' families are subject to the upheavals of moving from time to time. That can be trauma for some, but it wasn't for me. Especially in retrospect, it seems to me to have presented a golden opportunity. It meant starting over again, leaving behind a portion of one's history, and blazing new trails. In 1934 I was eleven and we moved to another pastoral charge. I was excited by the prospects. An unexpected bonus was that in the new school, four grades to a room, there were only three children in grade 6 into which I would normally enter. Two of these had not impressed the teacher with their aptitude for study, and my report card suggested a marked contrast with them. With the third member of the class I was promoted to grade 7 without spending a day in grade 6, and before long we two were contenders for the leadership of our new class.

I also discovered that the small high school, in softball competition with neighboring communities, was lacking an effective pitcher. With my left hand delivery and my speed, also a credible batting record, I was playing on the high school team before I entered high school.

Meanwhile I was having some thoughts about myself and my conduct. I had decided by the age of twelve that smoking was not becoming to a Christian, least of all to a minister's son. I resolved to desist, and that I did. I was also aware how my language had little to differentiate it from that of my companions. Having resolved with success to abandon smoking, I subsequently resolved to clean up my language, and I proceeded to do so.

To the best of my knowledge neither of these decisions were communicated to my parents, for I don't think they were aware of the nature or the extent of these youthful exploits. If the inspiration came from outside myself, I would think participation in summer boys' camps, under church auspices, may have moved me in this direction. Later I was to make a conscious resolve to improve my grammar.

Father became more a part of my consciousness during this time. I can't say whether he devoted more time to my brother and me and to our friends, however. In any case, I was conscious of his efforts. He was leader for a group of boys known in church and community as Trail Rangers. As part of that program we were introduced to an adult view of sexuality, one which was factual, straightforward, and interesting. I remember some personal embarrassment over my father's venture into sex education. After all, what other father would do such a thing?

Toward the end of the four years that we lived in Clanwilliam, Manitoba, my sexual awakening was intensified. I was interested in girls, and I liked to tease them. But it was in another direction that my experience developed. A friend my own age invited me to spend the weekend with him on his family farm. Through him I was introduced to masturbation. Nocturnal emissions soon were part of my physical development, and despite the openness to conversation about sex displayed by my father, I preferred to struggle with my guilt rather than confide in him.

In yet another way I was moving toward his more adult world. I had been playing hockey, a sport which can rouse anxiety when glasses are involved. At age fourteen I yielded to my mother's persuasion and agreed to give up hockey if I could take up curling, the winter sport of adults in the community. My father prevailed on the board of the curling club to admit me as the first junior member. Thereafter two or three other boys also joined.

In a more serious vein, my political conscience began to form because of an event at home. In 1935 there was a general election in Canada. Some time prior to the election a couple of men called on my father. They talked long and earnestly. After they had gone I learned of their mission. Because of his sympathy and active support of the United Farmers of Manitoba, members of that organization deemed my father a suitable candidate for the newly formed C.C.F. (Canadian Commonwealth Federation), the socialist party born of poverty in the Canadian west. Though several of his colleagues in the ministry did stand for election and he was a convinced supporter of the social gospel, as it was then described, he declined to stand for nomination. I was disappointed.

The reason for his decision, as I understood it, was the conviction that the Christian church was a more strategic and worthwhile arena for his endeavor. The Oxford Group Movement was spreading, holding out a means to transform relationships and advance the kingdom of God. In this

35

environment, and without any family pressure but with every evidence of goodwill on their part, I professed my faith in Christ and was received into full Communion at age fourteen.

The next move was to Winnipeg. The year was 1938. I don't know all the reasons for that move, but I was very much aware of one of them. I was in grade 10 in a one-room country high school. Though there was some discussion of and I had some interest in banking as a career, there was also a strong concern that there be access to higher education in case I should wish it. There was no way a rural minister's salary could support that eventuality, so the obvious solution was to move to the big city.

My father was never a person to go out and sell himself. He preferred to rely on a "call" or "to be settled" as he understood the Presbyterian and Methodist traditions. This time, however, perhaps yielding to mother's persuasion, he actively sought a call and ended with the necessity of choosing between two struggling causes, both serving essentially laboring people in areas of high unemployment. I looked forward to the change. Nor can I recall any regrets at the time. In retrospect, I can see how profound were some of the consequences.

I was a fairly intelligent country boy, accustomed to being a leader in school and something of a star in school sports. I came to a huge city high school, the forty-eighth boy in an all-male class, many of whom had been together throughout their school life. Many of them were articulate and bright in the classroom and adept at school sports, chief of which were basketball, which I had never known, and football, which to that point I had not distinguished from soccer. Moreover, I was a year younger than most of my classmates and my home was geographically isolated from the neighborhood where most of them lived.

The more constant part of my experience centered around the church, the Sunday services, the Sunday school, Boy Scouts, and special events. My mind was questioning many of the traditional beliefs, but I felt a real sense of belonging and I liked to sing. Even when no other part of the service seemed to speak to me, I still liked to attend. The sermons sometimes produced, directly or indirectly, an emotional response. Like the Sunday in 1940 when patriotism was running high and my father in his sermon dared to suggest that Britain, its allies, and our own nation stood under the judgment of God as surely as Nazi Germany. Controversy erupted immediately in the congregation which had numerous British immigrants. I was loyal to my father. He seemed so right and yet to speak the truth seemed so dangerous.

There was another emotional Sunday. Though I had my doubts about His divinity, I had an intense feeling for the example of the man Jesus. On this particular Sunday I came home to burst into tears. The agony within stemmed from my conflict over passivism, with which I identified Jesus and to whom I felt committed, and the compelling logic of resisting tyranny and oppression so manifest in the world of that date. I wanted to be a soldier (I was then seventeen), and I also wanted to follow Jesus. How could I do both?

Through the church and through music, I was drawn into the company of a young lady whom I think of as my first girlfriend. I was seventeen. She was a year and a half older. We were part of a youth group at church. We enjoyed each other's company but our activities were quite limited. For one thing I had no money. For another, each of us was living at home and subject to the restraints of parents who took their responsibilities seriously. For my part, I had my strong commitment to responsible behavior, which permitted some adventure into new experiences but with very definite limits. Over much of a year we saw each other regularly. Then summer employment took me away for a time. When we met again I was not ready to resume the relationship. There was an emotional scene suggesting that she had invested much more in our future than I had. I was concerned for her, was fearful lest the upset be damaging to her, but was determined that we should not continue together. It was over, and I was relieved.

Vocationally there was much uncertainty. I was heading for college but World War II was in progress. I was too young to enlist, but I expected I would use my mathematical ability in the Royal Canadian Artillery some day. In the background was the likelihood of becoming a mathematics teacher. In my sophomore year, still too young for military service or even for compulsory military training, I volunteered for the latter only to find that my eyesight put me in the category "unfit for military service." With that changed prospect, the future seemed to organize around teaching school and getting into politics. My interest in politics and especially in socialism prompted me to major in economics. The economic paralysis and the widespread poverty of the thirties and the chaos of global war seemed to cry out for solutions. I was confident that Christian love expressed through political action could deliver the world from its enemy.

Being a minister's son I frequently had to defend my decision not to follow in my father's footsteps. I did so, at times vehemently. I didn't like the deprivations, controversies, and restraints of being a minister. I didn't want my kids to be preacher's kids. And to some I also admitted that I couldn't be a minister because I felt I was a heretic. I didn't believe some things which I took to be basic and was sometimes emphatic in my unbelief, and I had doubts about some other doctrines.

Enrolled in liberal arts at a church college, I found many of my classmates were preparing themselves for the ministry. My closest associations at college were with these and, my parents having moved from the city, my social life centered in a big city church and its young people's group, in which students from the college took a leading part. Through such associations I was asked to teach a Sunday school class in a city mission. The church, in my experience, had a lot to offer me: other young people away from home, the dispossessed of the city, the sufferers of the war-torn world. And I was part of the church, although disqualified in my own eyes because of my doubts and disbelief. I can't remember any pain because of this. In fact, I think I was relieved by possession of an irrefutable excuse for not facing the claims of the ministry as a vocation.

Another summer's employment brought me face to face with a theological student. He was also at that time a conscientious objector and, being older and of an age for military service, had already suffered considerable abuse for his adherence to his conscience. He impressed me with his intelligence, his sincerity, and his courage. More than that, he was very open with me in acknowledging that he had his doubts and his reservations about many aspects of the faith and, further, that among theological students he was not alone in this. The handwriting was on the wall then, though I was not really aware of it. Some months later, after much conscious assessment of what gifts I had to offer through the ministry, and nothing approximating the traditional experience of a "call," I offered myself and was accepted as a candidate for the ministry just prior to my nineteenth birthday. My first thought was not of a parish ministry but of becoming a missionary overseas. Later I was to explore the possibility of combining theology and medicine but was dissuaded by church policy at that time.

The theological seminary which I entered, adjunct to the college I had attended, was very small. My class, larger than most, numbered twelve. I was one of two students considerably younger than the rest. My grades usually placed me in the top 25 percent of the class, but I often felt that the older students were giving and receiving more than I. My fellows elected me "high priest" in my senior year of seminary, but it seemed to me the result of a default rather than recognition of my particular gifts. The office required me to deal with faculty from time to time. I felt that I was received with dignity and respect but that their world and my world were far apart. The involvement in the seminary community was apparent but the fruits of that involvement left me far from satisfied.

The war was coming to a close. Already some veterans were returning to college and seminary. Some candidates for the ministry already had wives. Some had children. I married in my senior year of seminary. I believe I was the second to do so while in attendance at the seminary. I had met my wife-to-be when she was attending teachers' college. She was part of the same young people's group at the church. She was also in the choir. I really hadn't noticed her until long after she had noticed me, perhaps because in war time there was a dearth of single young males and an abundance of interesting and attractive young women. In that context it was not hard for a young man to become something of a leader and to be seen as such. Her name was Margaret, born of immigrant Scottish parents who had taken up farming in Manitoba. She had lived all her life in a small rural community where church and school were centers of community life. Her mother was an organist in the village church. From childhood Margaret had looked forward to teaching school. Immediately on graduation she joined the Winnipeg teaching staff as a primary teacher.

We found we had the same ideals of service, similar commitments to the Christian faith, and respect for family traditions which appeared to be similar. Neither of us had been accustomed to much money. We found many things we enjoyed together. We were attracted to each other, discovered the power of sexual desires, and struggled with the restraints born of the view that sexual fulfillment is to be reserved for marriage.

For Margaret the idea of being a minister's wife was a challenge not to be accepted quickly. For me, my momentary hesitation was a critical one: Could Margaret accept the possibility that, in obedience to my understanding of the will of God, we might live on an isolated Indian reserve? After a period of crisis, she decided that she could.

Following my ordination we were posted to Nelson House, an Indian settlement in remote northern Manitoba. During my seminary days, I had been confronted by the deplorable conditions facing our native Indians and could not justify thought of overseas mission service with such crying needs so close at hand. I had volunteered for Indian mission work. A school teacher was also required. Margaret was appointed. We entered the work as partners. She taught school. I was the missionary. We shared household tasks from laundry to baking bread. I was also deputy for the Indian Agent, dispenser of medicines, registrar of vital statistics, and ombudsman.

Two noteworthy features of those three years stand out. First, through reading all the submissions to the special committee of the House of Commons studying the Indian Act, I became acquainted with the values of self-help as an objective and with the methods of community development. I protested inwardly against the paternalism which I saw everywhere in relation to the Indian people, and outwardly, I worked in very autocratic fashion for self-determination along lines acceptable to me! Second, the comparative isolation allowed time for reading. I first learned of CPE through journals and read whatever I could about pastoral skills and counseling techniques. I nurtured a dream that some day I would seek training.

With active encouragement from my superintendent, after three yars I responded to the shortage of ministers in the church by accepting a call to a rural pastorate. Then, after four years, the lures of the city took me to an expanding suburban church. Again after four years, I yielded to entreaties to return to northern Manitoba as pastor in a strategic northern community. The decision was made with the realization that to move at that time was really to renounce all thought of any extended period of graduate study in my chosen field of pastoral care. With a wife and three sons to support, with very limited income, how could I ever finance such a venture?

My parish experiences were indeed varied. I have already made reference to the years on the Indian reserve. My rural pastorate was a rewarding one from my standpoint. A positive response to what was a church-centered ministry to the community seemed obvious. My suburban pastorate saw me submerged in the life of the parish with no other involvement apart from the church. My last pastorate was a ministry to the whole community using the church as a base and including what might be considered politics on the local level, such as integration of Indian education with the town school, improved law enforcement, representations to the government on behalf of community needs.

I was aware, though I seldom acknowledged it, of some disquiet within me regarding my ministry. I was bothered by the controlling way in which I had tried to move persons toward self-help. I was not comfortable with the way in which persons who had borne the burden and heat of the day had been inundated by the flood of newcomers who responded to my ministry and outflanked or overpowered those who opposed changes very acceptable to me. I was not satisfied with my handling of a major crisis in my suburban congregation involving junior and senior choirs in which a number of persons were hurt. I further blamed myself for not being able to move the congregation into further building in the face of needs which were so obvious to me. As for my last parish, I felt that much had been accomplished despite real problems not of my doing; but I also felt that the basic problems were far from resolved and wondered whether I had the competence to deal with them. Then, it was 1960, wonder of wonders, miracle of miracles, and strange as it might seem, the way opened up for me to undertake twelve weeks of Clinical Pastoral Education in Houston, Texas. The dream, long unfulfilled, was about to be realized. With our four boys we headed south. Feeling that my strength was in one-to-one relationships, because of the response to my faithful visiting of the sick, I set out to test my strength and stake out the potential for me in this kind of training.

It was a glorious summer. I worked long and hard Monday through Friday. The weekends were reserved for the family. And how warmly we were received! How exhilarating the new country! Texas, the fabulous state!

At the end of the summer we headed back to Manitoba intent on bending our efforts to return the following year for an extended program of Clinical Pastoral Education. I had been judged the most advanced of my class in pastoral function and was actively encouraged to continue. As for me, I was gratified, but I was also star-gazer. How competent my supervisors and professors were! How much I would like to be like them!

III

I Know I'm Helping, but Should I Be Doing More?

I returned as planned in the fall of the following year for an intern year. My wife and I had acquired by adoption an infant daughter long sought, so we arrived in Houston with our family of five, with meager financial resources, an additional limitation on my wife's capacity to supplement our income, but with a ready circle of personal support to encourage us. I had all of the confidence which stemmed from a long-standing desire, the affirmation of the previous summer, and the providential way in which events seemed to be unfolding before us.

My clinical assignment was the Veterans Administration Hospital, the psychiatric section and, specifically, the only female ward. It was viewed as a good placement because, while having only thirty-five patients, it had a cross section of the common psychiatric categories. My prior experience of psychiatric hospitals was virtually nil, my exposure to psychiatric patients minimal; nothing on an extended or intensive basis. It was a strange world for me, not without its threats. I was encouraged to take my own time in getting acquainted, to meet staff, to browse over medical records, to take my own initiatives in meeting patients. I ventured forth from the protection of the nursing station slowly.

The first conversation which I had with a patient was uneventful in itself. It had little depth and served only as a springboard for the second. Inquiring about the name of another patient nearby I was accommodated with the added comment: "She may talk to you. She won't talk to us."

The threat in those words was not sufficient to deter me. I introduced myself as a newcomer and a chaplain. Right away we were in conversation for my identity as a Canadian was soon apparent and, by happy coincidence, the patient in a brief interlude out of the hospital had made a vacation trip by bus to British Columbia. In fact, it was immediately upon her return that she had realized that all was not well for her, and she had been readmitted to the hospital a short time before our meeting, at her own request.

A subsequent visit established the fact that I was in a training program though I was a minister with some years of experience, and that my visits with patients were subject to supervision. I was there to learn through my efforts to minister. She seemed quite interested.

The chief instrument for supervision in CPE, as mentioned previously, is the verbatim report. It is not the transcript of a recording, as might be possible in a counseling service by arrangement with the client. It is a construct from memory of what took place during a pastoral visit: time, place, appearance, mood of the participants, the actual dialogue as accurately as possible, including reference to feeling and nonverbal clues along with the words exchanged. Usually, a brief outline is set down soon after the visit is completed. Then, within twenty-four hours or so, the outline is fleshed out, analyzed, and evaluated by the student for submission to a chaplain supervisor. That report becomes the basis for a personal conference with the supervisor, and frequently is presented also for consideration by a group of the student's peers. The supervisor, by the way, is recognized as such at the end of a rigorous certification process.

I chose to write up one of my early conversations with Mrs. Jones. Because she seemed so ready, even eager, to talk to me, because the early relationship showed signs of dealing with significant issues, and because I hoped to accumulate written data which might be useful for a thesis concerning some as yet undetermined issue in pastoral care, I sought and received permission to write up a continuous account of my efforts to minister to her. Over a period of seven months I wrote up thirty-six such reports. Because she welcomed and accepted me as a minister, because she accepted for herself the role of facilitator of my learning, and because she has subsequently encouraged me to write this book, I can share with you these glimpses of our relationship and reflections on the happenings which transpired between us.

I invite you to form your own opinions as to what took place and the dynamics which might account for the same. In what sense was it ministry? The setting was a hospital. Could the doctor or the social worker have done the same thing? If not exclusive to the clergy, could a Christian without professional training in ministry have brought the requisite gifts to bear in such a relationship? What was really involved in this helpful experience for the patient? Helpful it was from her standpoint at that time. Helpful it was as she has viewed it in retrospect. Helpful it seemed to me at that time and to more objective viewers who knew of it then. In what ways was I servant to her or minister of the Lord Jesus Christ?

Without further data it is possible to identify as significant the fact that I came to her. That is a common characteristic of the professional ministry. Pastoral initiative has commonly distinguished professional ministry from the service of most other professionals, though that is no longer as true as it used to be. Among Christians the professional has no monopoly on initiative.

Another significant factor in the beginning would seem to have been the fact that I was identified by role as a chaplain or minister. Mrs. Jones, as noted earlier, was not given to talking with just anyone. It is conceivable that she received me as she did because I was a man. The ward, except for the doctor and a social worker, was all female. Subsequent reporting of her experiences and attitude toward men all but rules out that possibility. Moreover, it became apparent very early that she identified herself with a Christian tradition and had some perceptions of ministers and expectations concerning them. Though her experience of them was somewhat ambiguous, on balance, it seemed that she should accord them respect and possibly even trust. I felt comfortable in my role as minister. I accepted her acceptance of me with ease. I cashed in on her predisposition, one of the advantages of being not just a Christian but a pastor.

The role also had its disadvantages, for ministers do represent different traditions and a variety of attitudes and practices. This was illustrated in the first verbatim record of our relationship. It is reproduced in full, in part to show you essentially where I started in my counseling and listening skills, in part because it clearly shows the nature of the patient's thinking and hopes, no doubt already projected onto me. It also shows the kind of process encouraged in CPE by way of analysis and evaluation, and shows that while I could acknowledge my own limitations in the encounter, I was not eager to be the subject of close scrutiny or to explore the dynamics of my own behavior.

The setting: The patient was seated before the television in the lounge of the hospital ward but did not appear to be watching the program. She is medium height, very thin in appearance and looks more than her thirty-nine years, neat and very self-conscious, tending to look down a good deal. She looked up and smiled at the chaplain's approach.

C-1   "Mrs. Jones, I haven't been speaking with you for a few days. How is it going?"

P-1   (In a pleasant soft-spoken voice) "Oh, about the same."

C-2   "You don't notice much change?"

P-2   "No, I don't (with a voice of quiet resignation but without obvious hopelessness). I've been here for four months, and I feel just about the same."

C-3   "Does this mean that you have some days when you feel real good and other days when you feel kind of bad?"

P-3 "No. I had problems when I came in, and I still have them."

C-4 "I think I understand."

P-4 "What denomination did you say you were?" (I had a feeling that she had been waiting for a chance to ask this question. There was no sense of awkwardness following my response and no feeling that she was trying to escape my questioning. Several questions and responses followed in quick succession about the chaplain's denomination. Then . . .) "Do you have confession in your church, (with some hesitation) like the Catholics?"

C-5 "No. We believe that there is value in confession, sharing with another person if that person is understanding. But that is not like Catholic confession. Why did you ask that?"

P-5 "I know some Catholic girls and they seem to be quite different after they confess. They can go and do the same thing again then go and confess."

C-6 "You feel that this really does something for them?"

P-6 "Yes, I do. It seems to do them a lot of good (wistfully)."

P-7 "I don't think it is the same to talk to somebody who is not a priest or a man of the cloth. The doctors say that confession is good, therapeutic, they say, but I don't think so. Only God can forgive."

C-7 "I'm wondering if you feel that this may be part of your problem. You don't feel that you can get all of the help that you need from the doctors? Can you talk with the doctor freely or are there some things that you just can't share with him?"

P-8 "Yes, I can talk with him alright . . . no, there are some things that I can't tell him (hesitantly)."

C-8 "Tell me, have you ever been involved in a church where you could confide in the minister?"

48

P-9   "No, I haven't had much to do with any church. I was converted in a Baptist church and attended for a little while. But then I dropped out. I really don't know much about any church."

C-9   "Well, I would like you to feel that if you would like to talk further with me about any of your troubles you may do just that. (The patient showed some signs of hesitation, as if trapped.) I know that is a big decision to make. I didn't intend to put you on the spot. It's something you may want to think about for some time. I'll be around the ward most afternoons."

Evaluation

Rapport was good. The patient showed signs of welcoming the visit and assumed the initiative to raise the matter she wanted to talk about. The chaplain was over-anxious, however, and was premature in offering to act as confessor. The relationship could have been seriously set back though a subsequent conversation would indicate that no great damage was done.

The patient has had long periods of hospitalization over the past few years. She is presently well orientated and can talk psychotherapy with some intelligence. She keeps pretty much to herself, communicates very little, and seems to have little sign of motivation for recovery. Unless this pattern can be changed, she will remain a chronic schizophrenic.

Although she demonstrates the self-consciousness and guilt which goes with a low opinion of herself, she has enough pride in her to feel that she knows better than the doctor, at least with reference to confession. Of course, she may be right! But she lacks an adequate understanding of the gospel and no confession is going to help her unless in some way the love of God is experienced through her problem. Either way, future plans should include active interest and support with attention to her feelings so that she may experience acceptance and forgiveness as and when the need arises.

C-2 is an acceptable response. It shows attention to what she has said, conveys my understanding of what she had shared. A more complete listening response would have picked up not only what she had said but how she had said it. The pleasant voice with which she spoke might have conveyed that she was not complaining. If that were so it would be worthy of note, whether reported back to her or not. In any case, my response was such as to encourage her to elaborate or explain and to take the initiative wherever she wanted to go.

I took the initiative with C-3, wanting to know more of her experience. I had reached out to her with a desire to help, and how could I do so without more information? It wasn't forthcoming. In C-4 I conceded a momentary defeat.

Much to my surprise and delight, coupled with a dash of chagrin, (should counselors or pastors end up talking about themselves?) she took the initiative at P-4. My parenthesis in the verbatim was inspired by the theory that persons sometimes take the initiative in order to escape from emotions associated with the subject in hand. That had stayed with me from the reading of Harry Stack Sullivan's *The Psychiatric Interview*.[1] It seemed to me that she had asked her question for reasons independent of any agenda that I might have.

Her question to me was a bit of a problem. I had the information she requested, but I knew from reading and previous discussion with others that back of the question there well might be a purpose to be served which would not be achieved through mere information. The appropriate response, therefore, might not be the information per se, but more specific information addressed to the concern which lay back of the question.

With some uncertainty and discomfort, therefore, I gave the information, then asked the reason for the question. My answer did not intimidate or deter her. P-5 is quite revealing and my response, while not as complete as it might have been, allowed her to continue. She told me about Catholic girls but I also heard wistfulness in P-6. Then there was additional data to deal with, theories about confession, attitudes toward doctors, and toward God. Why hadn't I said in response to P-5, "You wish you had someone to confess to?" She might have agreed and gone on to tell me of her church experience and of her failure to find a confessor. Instead, (C-7) I was intent on finding out what limitations she experienced in confessing to her doctors.

The role I assumed was that of problem-solver. My next participation is confirmation of that. If she couldn't deal with all her concerns under medical auspices that suggested an open door for a man of the cloth. I didn't want to seem naive and offer my services without checking to see what her experience of ministers might be. I don't know that I was encouraged by the evidence of her isolation from the church, but having raised the issue as directly as I had, I felt bound to offer myself as a confessor, whatever that might mean to her. I felt the challenge but was daunted by her apparent hesitation. My need to be needed and attempts to identify for her a confessor obscured her clear statement, pathetic in its hopelessness, "Only God can forgive" (P-6). The next visit was initiated by the patient who asked about my involvement in group therapy and reported her own experience:

P-1   "It didn't do me much good (with a laugh). The other patients were too aggressive for me."

C-1   "That sometimes happens in groups. A few do most of the talking."

What does this suggest about ministry? It points to the growing mutuality in the relationship. Mrs. Jones felt free to initiate. Her initiative may have been related to my role, however, there was nothing overtly pertaining to a religious concern. It was personal. It was sharing a little bit of herself, her experience, and her perception of herself. Instead of responding to her as person, I contented myself with normalizing her experience and sharing my experience and knowledge of groups. When personal sharing is met by generalization and depersonalization the inevitable follows: Silence. That is what happened. Her initiative was dead.

I eventually broke the silence by harking back to the previous conversation in which she had made reference to her conversion. It might be described as an attempt to get a religious history. I was wanting information and, consciously, I was also interested in her feelings as they had been at an earlier point in her life. Why such an interest? My perception, it would seem, was that her present could only be understood by reference to her past and, beyond that, perhaps because I was reading Freud at the time, I was impressed by the dynamics of repressed emotions and his claims that the way to freedom was through abreaction, the reexperiencing of the repressed with all its force. I was also sensitized to the fact that I was a chaplain on the ward, not a psychiatrist or a psychologist or a social worker, but a clergyman. Hence my selective response to a patient with a known religious interest. I had my agenda. I needed information in order to help. She needed to emote, and I might provide the occasion in a field uniquely the domain of my calling.

Mrs. Jones was ready to comply but, unexpectedly we came upon some limits:

P-1   "That was about two years, 1951 to 1953. Then something happened, but I can't talk about that."

C-1   "I understand. (pause) But whatever it was it was of such a nature as to discourage you from seeking out any other church?"

P-2   "Two years ago when I was in . . . I went to the church to see about getting my letter. The pastor said they would restore my membership if I came forward again, and then they would give me my letter. But I never did anything about it. (pause) Does your church do things that way?"

I reported factually. Mrs. Jones made no comment about my reply. She went on to report her dismay over a situation where a man had been "read out of the church," and she pressed me as to whether my church did things like that. I felt the pressure, could not make an outright denial, and was unhappy about my attempt to hedge. She continued to press.

P-11 "Does your church believe in baptism by immersion?"

C-11 "Either way is acceptable in our denomination."

P-12 "The Bible says that Jesus was baptized by immersion." (When there was no immediate response she went on.) "I like to think that my way is the right way."

C-12 "That is perfectly natural. I have the feeling you have given this and similar matters a good deal of thought."

As I look at this encounter now I conclude that I was aware of her sensitivity to disclosure of painful material, and I respected her right not to tell me about it. Her reticence on that point did not deter me from pursuing my agenda. She responded and moved on to less sensitive areas about which she had, nonetheless, real concern. Her pointed questions to me were thinly veiled expressions of current feelings. I treated them as requests for information. They were too hot to handle. Could I tell her that I upheld the need for discipline in the body of Christ? What else could I do but give a factual answer? I didn't know how to deal with her feelings. Perhaps she sensed my vulnerability, not taking issue with my answers, which were intended to be conciliatory, but pressing on to raise another issue of potential disagreement. Was she testing my orthodoxy? Would she write me off if I disagreed with her? Or was she testing me to see if I would read her out of the church? I am convinced that it was the latter. It was in this same context, I believe, that she identified herself as accepting the five fundamentals. Though her stance could have involved me in a doctrinal debate, I accepted her statements as important to her. I expressed neither assent nor dissent. She promptly referred to the theme of expulsion from the church and expressed herself as favoring a church which did not have such a practice.

The relationship was not harmed. Indeed, I believe, it was strengthened as a result of this testing. There were opportunities missed, however, because of my confused view of my role and my still dormant awareness of what could be done with the patient's current feelings. By the same token, I had some awareness of my own feelings. I felt genuinely accepting of Mrs. Jones, eager to minister, encouraged by the developing relationship. I was less aware of the intensity of my desire to accomplish something and of my frustration with the superficiality, the hesitancy, the disruptions, and the silences which characterized so much of our time together. Nor was I aware of how much I contributed to that result. I may have had some vague notions pointing in that direction, but they were excluded from my consciousness.

Two days later, Mrs. Jones met me in the hall. She held a New Testament in her hand. She initiated the conversation with a biblical and theological question, "What is the 'millenium' and where do you read about it in the New Testament?" It was obvious she wanted to pursue her relationship with me. I welcomed that, even while I felt disappointed that she did do so through this indirect and impersonal way. I also felt ill prepared to discuss the "millenium" because it played little part in my own religious experience, and I knew that for many Christians it had great potential for divisiveness. I expressed a willingness to discuss the subject with her and proposed that we find a place to sit down.

C-1   "I've been thinking about your question. I'm curious to know why you asked it. This is important to you?"
P-2   "No, not really. Just curious."
C-3   "What do you think the millenium is all about?"
P-3   "Isn't Christ supposed to reign for a thousand years and there will be peace on earth?"

C-4   "I think you are right . . . that is part of it. But I think there must be a reason why this idea interests you."

P-4   (Laughing) "You sound just like the doctors do."

C-5   "In what way?"

P-5   "Oh, they always want to know why."

Pause

P-7   "I think the world is pretty wicked. Don't you? I don't think that God can let it go on much longer. Do you?"

C-7   "How does this make you, yourself, feel?"

P-8   "Well, I'm nearly 40. And I have tried to do the right thing. I have done about all I can do."

C-8   "Do you mean that it doesn't worry you because you feel you have done your best?"

P-9   "That's right. I know God is a God of mercy and love. But I also know that he is a judge, and it frightens me just a little sometimes. I don't worry about it, though. I just feel that if I have to go to hell, there is nothing I can do about it but accept it."

C-9   "Just resign yourself to it. Is that it?"

P-17   "I have done three or four things which are . . . real bad. I think I am forgiven . . . but I don't know."

C-17   "You feel some real uncertainty about these things?"

P-18   "I have real strong faith but sometimes all I can do is hope. . . . Do you think it is possible to know that you have been saved?"

C-18   "I don't think you can ever prove it, but I do think it is possible to grow more sure of the mercy and the love of God."

P-19   "I'd like to think so. I know you are supposed to have faith in him and feel reverent toward him, but sometimes I feel resentful and angry and rebellious against him."

C-19   "You feel that such feelings are not as they should be."

P-20   "I don't think so . . . but I do feel that way . . . sometimes. Like Job, I guess."

C-20   "Job felt pretty strongly against God, didn't he? Well, it's five o'clock. You will be missing your supper and I must go."

P-24   "Can we meet again and discuss the milennium?"

C-24   "Why, of course."

P-25   "Would you say a prayer for me?"

C-25   "Usually I ask a person what in particular they would like me to pray for. Do you have any suggestions?"

P-26   "I would like you to pray for my soul."

The Prayer: O God, whom we know through Jesus Christ who has taught us to call thee Our Father, who knowest our secret thoughts yet lovest us with an everlasting love, look upon this Thy child and bestow Thy grace upon her that she may know Thy love and find her place in fellowship with Thee both now and forever. In Jesus name, Amen.

Though I had been subjected to many direct questions before and had responded to the content in a direct way, and had suffered no ill effects that I was aware of, I was nonetheless resistant to more of the same kind. I didn't object overtly, nor did I express my preference for some alternate way of relating. Instead I made a persistent effort to get into the personal and to avoid a direct answer to her questions. C-1 and 2 were attempts to get at the context of her questioning. C-3 was avoidance, turning the question back to her. C-4 was a very modest concession to her agenda with yet another attempt to get on with mine.

Her laughter (P-4) seems to indicate a growing ease and acceptance of me. I could accept her as a person despite some doctrinal views to which she adhered strongly. She, for her part, could accept this man of the cloth who sounded "just like the doctors do," not wanting to answer direct questions with direct answers. From another standpoint it was a stalemate. I frustrated her desires, and she as powerfully frustrated mine. Not to the point of no return, however, the process continued. Not skilled in recognizing or responding to the emotional, I struggled to find ways of dealing with her questions and ideas, sensing the inadequacies of answers to effect change, yet knowing of no alternative. I bought in to the role of being a problem-solver or a healer nonetheless and intermittently drew on the stock-in-trade which was at hand: my theological concepts and my knowledge of the church and the world primarily, and my very elementary knowledge of a variety of therapeutic approaches. I expressed views, offered leading questions, recognized the urge and the futility of argument, but did not see the relevance or have the freedom to share my own deep sense of hopelessness and futility as I struggled to discover what ministry should be. I recognized and tried to work with her feelings of quiet resignation, self-doubt, and fear, not realizing that in these very experiences was a basis for mutuality and the potential for healing.

One last comment on this session: Her perception of me as a Christian and as a minister suggested to her not only the appropriateness of religious topics for discussion but also of prayer. I had not initiated that subject. Now she did by asking me to pray for her.

I followed a technique which I had just acquired, enlisting the help of the person who had requested the prayer by asking for specific concerns to be included. Her immediate response was: "I would like you to pray for my soul." That was too general for my liking, but I felt I had to accept her simple response and therefore offered a very general prayer for her, representing my understanding of her need. Would I do the same now? I don't know.

The next conversation was not set down in verbatim form. The record is a summary only.

Mrs. Jones reported that the ward physician had that morning discouraged her from thinking of early discharge. "Too tense, not ready yet," he said. She accepted the verdict with resignation. "The doctor knows best." I pursued current feelings, and these included her feelings about medication. They seemed to produce a devil-may-care attitude. "I have a problem with gossip," which being interpreted means "people are talking about me." "Drugs help you to feel 'so what.' " She expressed the view that drugs lead to lowering of moral standards but insisted that this wasn't true of her.

I switched the subject away from moral standards by asking if medication helped her to be at ease in talking with other people, with me for instance. Her response was to the effect that I seemed relaxed and that, more than medication, helped her.

Back, not to the effect of medication but to the problem of gossip. I wanted to know if this problem continued. She admitted it did, then went on to offer an explanation given by psychiatrists, that this problem is associated with guilt. She talked of the guilt she experienced surrounding the failure of her marriage and went on to say that she felt forgiven for these sins. I noted that she still seemed to experience guilt even though forgiven. For this she had a ready explanation. She had been forgiven and "lived well" for several years after, but then had "fallen again and again," so often, in fact, that she was fearful about ever being able to "live the pure life again." Her hope seemed to be in discharge, a job, the chaste life with no thoughts of remarriage. She had, in her view, defeated God's purpose in not having a family, and she would not defy his will again, which she deemed she would be doing if she were to marry again. Her conviction was that she would have to stay away from men or she would find herself again in the position where she would be too weak to do the right thing.

The session ended with this prayer:

Oh, God, our Heavenly Father, who has made us for Thyself, both male and female according to Thy purpose, grant us to know Thy will. O Thou who didst send Thy son into the world while we were yet sinners, give us grace that we may not only know Thy love, but walk before Thee in newness of life through Jesus Christ Our Lord, Amen.

I can offer no sure explanation for the summary report. It may be that too much time had elapsed between the conversation and the attempt to reconstruct it. Hence there is no way of assessing why or how Mrs. Jones was able to share so much of herself in this session. She began with a current experience, with information, and a passive personal response. She ended with the same lifeless resignation. While she nourished some hope, it was weak and unsure. The alternatives she saw were narrowly prescribed, her vulnerability very much part of her consciousness. Momentary diversions in the flow of the conversation, such as the effects of drugs on morals, her social relationship, and the currency of the gossip problem did not detract from her preoccupation with her future in this world.

I felt decidedly uncomfortable with her very tentative solution. It seemed so much like the solution she had tried before, but what could I say? What if I rejected her solution? What alternative could I suggest? I felt helpless, too. Fortunately, she wasn't asking me to tell her what she should do.

Approximately six weeks had lapsed up to this point. Our meetings had not been scheduled. They were chance meetings sometimes, or so it seemed. On occasion I would seek her out. Now we agreed that we should meet regularly. The initiative for this came from me. I should report that medically the patient was under the general oversight of the ward physician, and he had just assumed this role because previously the patient had been in the care of a psychiatric resident who had moved on to a neurological rotation. His intent was to continue with Mrs. Jones in psychotherapy. By this time it was apparent that this wasn't happening. With the knowledge and consent of the ward physician and of my own supervisor, I proceeded to structure our meetings. My stated purpose was "to give encouragement and support through exploring her feelings of the present and of the past insofar as they seem to have a bearing on her present and her future."

Another session began with the patient's interest in my activities. Again it led to sharing. The subject was group therapy and her reporting was that the other members were too aggressive for her, that she had never been competitive, that she had been afraid for her safety at times, and while it helped to know that others had similar problems, she had concluded that she was different. She related her fear in the face of anger in the group to her childhood experience of her parents fighting. While she was ambivalent about the merits of competition, she allowed that her rejection of it could reflect a weak ego (her term) and, with encouragement, she talked about her striving for a husband, a new home, and a car—achievements which had not brought her happiness. Moreover she said, she had a Christian friend who had a fine home and a family, and was happy, but who claimed that most people are not. She concluded wistfully: "I'm happy, but I'm sick . . . and I don't know why."

My perception of my responses is that they were of two kinds; reporting of understandings gained and invitations to further elaborations concerning feelings identified. For example, she seemed to suggest that her current troubles stemmed from the sin of birth control.

C-20   "You have told me when you were practicing it you thought it was quite the right thing to do. But for some reason your view changed. Any idea when or why?"

P-20   "I know when and why (with a wry smile), but I can't tell you about that."

C-21   "You can't?" (after a pause) "I can appreciate that this is a very personal matter to discuss with anyone, especially with a minister perhaps. But frankly, I'm curious. As a minister I'm very much interested in why you changed."

P-21   (Sheepishly, but without a great deal of hesitation) "Well, I heard a voice tell me that it was wrong."

C-22   "You find it hard to speak about this special message?"

P-22   "I don't have hallucinations, but I know that birth control is wrong. I never told the doctors about this. They would just laugh and say that everybody does it."

The issue of right and wrong and how one can be sure of God's will was faced in the same manner as other potentially contentious subjects, the patient holding to her view with varying degrees of emphasis, and the chaplain not taking a stand but allowing for the validity of other views. In fact, I did not agree with her view of birth control, and I think she sensed this.

P-25   "I feel much better now that I have told you. I felt better after our talk last week."

C-26   "Now that you have told me, do you think you may be able to tell the doctor?"

P-26   "I don't think I will. I think I'm through with doctors. I'll need their help to get out and get established, but I think this kind of counseling is more what I need."

C-27   "I don't understand."

P-27   "Well, you are a man of God, and you don't laugh at sin."

C-28   "I take your problem seriously even if you don't know what I think about it."

P-28   "That's right."

The personal nature of the sharing is apparent. In the early moments of this meeting the sharing was of a short staccato nature, but Mrs. Jones had abandoned her questioning of me. Hence I no longer had the problem, which I had experienced so much earlier, of trying to hunch what her questions were all about. I was better able to comprehend what she was really communicating. I was more accurate in my reporting of what I understood and when I did ask questions, as I continued to do, they were closer to the direction which her own dynamics were taking her. My stock-in-trade was still to focus on her feelings.

P-20 presented me with an unexpected problem. I didn't know what to do with it. Finally I decided to acknowledge her reticence and the naturalness of it, but to affirm the strength of my interest and to appeal to her interest in my professional growth. She overcame her sensitivity in reporting about the voice, something she had apparently kept back from her doctors. This illustrates the way patients do withhold information from persons who, in their experience, are apt to pass judgments, reject, or ridicule the behavior or the attitude revealed. From this standpoint, it is easier to tell a minister or a Christian about a voice than it is to tell a doctor. By the same token, it is more difficult to tell a minister the specifics of behavior representing some moral lapse which the minister may judge to be wrong, or which is thought to contravene the standards which he is assumed to uphold.

We had dealt with sensitive material, and she reported her good feelings about it. I had taken her seriously. I was less sensitive and responsive to the good feelings she reported then and there. Why did I pass them by? I was more alert to her history and her ideas and the implications these might have for her future. That I was future oriented is to be seen in the anxious concern. "Now that you have told me, do you think you will be able to tell the doctors?"

What would prompt such a leading question? It may have been my unconscious assumption that the doctor was the person who should be dealing with such deeply personal material, and that my pastoral role was secondary, facilitating what should happen in the other relationship. I know I was conscious of working in a psychiatric setting and such a definition of my role could be viewed as appropriate. It could also mean that subconsciously I had a departmentalized view of life. If not that, it might have meant that I was insecure in my relationship with the doctor and not wanting to test myself against him should he differ in his view of my proper sphere. There is the further possibility that I felt insecure in talking about sex with this woman of approximately my own age, though there was nothing about her appearance which attracted me to her, and I felt comfortable and secure in my marriage.

Mrs. Jones wasn't about to be led. She affirmed her enthusiasm for what she was experiencing with a minister. She did so with emphasis (P-25). She stood her ground in the face of my attempt to influence her in another direction.

I now see two points of failure in ministry in this exchange. I think I had some awareness of it then, but now I am fully convinced that one of the most important aspects of ministry is celebration. Christians have often been ready to reach out to persons in distress "to weep with those who weep." The other half of the mandate or call is "to rejoice with those who rejoice." The thanksgiving of the Eucharist, Holy Communion, is symbolic of the Christian's response to what God has done, not just in the sacrament or even through the historic events concerning Jesus Christ. It is a liturgical expression of praise for what God is even now doing for his people. I passed by her celebration in this instance because of my agenda. I had, and I have a struggle when I am involved, to accept thanks or appreciation when I am aware that there are objectives as yet unattained. My action implied that there would be time enough to celebrate when she was really healed.

The second failure was of a somewhat different order. When she persisted in her adherence to the importance of counseling with a minister, that is with me, she was celebrating our relationship. She was doing something else which I may have recognized but did not appreciate. She was affirming herself and her judgment against another opinion of what her priorities should be. It seemed to me to be what technically is called resistance, refusing to accept the help being offered, presumably by someone who knows better what is best for her. Had I recognized this as an evidence of strength, in a person whose passivity and helplessness seemed so marked, then I would have had cause to celebrate the discovery. We could have celebrated together, though the reason for doing so would have been different for each. Is there anything wrong about that? It is quite in keeping with

Christian orthodoxy I believe, for people bring very different experiences to the celebration of the Eucharist. That I did not realize this at the time I attribute to my own preoccupation, the problem of how to minister in a medical setting when the patient seems to be discounting the medical staff (P-26). My "now" took precedence over her "now," so I couldn't celebrate with her.

In retrospect, there are many places where I can affirm that the grace of God was operative, none more than here. Despite my limitations, it was plain that something significant was happening and that she attributed this to her relationship with me. This was gratifying, even though I could not be sure just how it was occurring or where it all would take us. I was hopeful, but hardly confident. The ward physician had been permissive but not at all encouraging when I had proposed giving major time and attention to Mrs. Jones. She had long been hospitalized. Her diagnosis was "chronic schizophrenic, paranoid type," and that meant a poor prognosis. He granted that she seemed responsive to me with her interest in confession, but he was satisfied that guilt was not her real problem. He even predicted that when her need to confess was exhausted she would have no further interest in me. At the same time he had to admit that something new was stirring in the patient. She had been the subject of just about every form of therapy in the past. More recently her physicians had been inclined to rely chiefly on medication for the alleviation of symptoms. Mrs. Jones' response to medication was limited, however. She was then on thorazine (largactal in Canada), medium to heavy dosage. Her response had been atypical inasmuch as most patients show weight gain. Without this, other clinical criteria of improvement tend to be minimized. Now, however, she was gaining weight. Her appetite was better. Her sleep patterns were more normal. She was participating in activities and was noticeably more sociable. He, nonetheless, anticipated an end to the improvement and a return to her earlier state, for reasons not understood but commonly observed. In the meantime there could be no denying the marked change from her earlier medical history. Why?

That question intrigued me. It still does. As I have looked back and forth over the entire relationship I have returned to this interview again and again. When I pressed her for some explanation for her strong preference for "this kind of counseling" she replied, "Well, you are a man of God, and you don't laugh at sin" (P-26). This suggests to me that she experienced herself as called to be a responsible person and knew that she had acted irresponsibly. She felt guilty because of her behavior. The doctors had not condemned her. They accepted her with her history. Whatever they thought of her behavior, whether they believed in sin or not, I doubt if she really knew, but she felt that they condoned her behavior and rejected her with her burden of guilt. She got the impression that she should be able to do whatever she felt like doing; do it and not feel guilty. It was as if what she did didn't matter. This she could not accept. Her efforts to move in this direction always resulted in more guilt and another failure. I might, or I might not agree with the rightness or wrongness of some of her past actions. She really didn't know. She did know however that I took her guilt seriously. My attitude, in effect, said "behavior does matter." However imperfectly it may have been expressed, she did feel accepted in the wholeness of her experience, including her guilt. It would seem that she had not encountered this before. Was this why her body could now utilize the medication?

The extent of her willingness to work with me was reflected, I think, when I came along with a request which must have been difficult for her, and she said yes. I asked her to participate in a case conference, in which I hoped she would allow herself to be interviewed by one of my professors before a group of my fellow students and fellow pastors. She agreed readily, even while reporting how difficult such experiences had been for her in the past. Invariably such a setting had led to tears. I wanted to understand her experience of tears if I could, and I asked questions of her. They led nowhere. After a pause I indicated that I would like to share an impression from our previous session. This seemed to me both natural and useful, and she accepted it that way. I suggested that she seemed more distressed by the interruption of her intended career than by the ending of her marriage. To my surprise she confirmed this, saying that she had earlier written off her marriage because of differences in goals and she and her husband's failure to achieve satisfaction in their sexual relations.

What followed was a conversation in which with great effort Mrs. Jones shared her distress about her sexual activity, her total lack of satisfaction in all such relationships, her conclusion that she must be asexual, and, though still afraid, her total lack of interest in sex now. She envied women in Holy Orders, for whom she assumed life was "pure and peaceful," even though it was her oft-repeated conviction that childbearing was the primary function of womanhood. In all this, religion seemed to be the source of her convictions.

In the same session, she introduced a related topic. "I have another question I wanted to ask you. Is it true that the Old Testament says that illegitimate children are forever barred from the Kingdom? Or does the New Testament say something different about them?" With great effort, she unfolded the background of her question—a pregnancy out of wedlock.

Throughout, my stance was essentially that of listening and support. I admitted to lack of knowledge and lack of certainty in response to some of her questions, and shared what knowledge or expertise as I had in a way which was suggestive rather than dogmatic. I was mildly confronting concerning Holy Orders as the solution to her sexual fears, but she seemed to experience no put-down for she moved on to a sensitive subject of her own choosing. In my evaluation of this visit I wrote:

"It is begining to look as if much of the patient's religious concern has been an afterthought, incorporating the values of hindsight;

further, that she is attempting to use religion in a repressive neurotic way. The chaplain should continue to facilitate confession and ultimately work toward a more healthy concept of religion. Her present concept of God is largely punitive, her understanding of the saving work of Christ is completely hidden if not, in fact, nonexistent despite her profession."

The sexual theme had prominence next session, beginning with reference to the Bible passage I had suggested for her reading. The initiative came from her, but I made an observation about the depth of her feelings when talking about her son as compared with other topics. At that point she agreed but announced that she wanted to talk about her relationships with men. Having said so she led off:

P-2   "Do you feel that sex offenses can be forgiven?"

(The chaplain looked at her seriously for a moment, then broke into a grin.)

C-2   "Now what are you wanting me to say?" (We have made something of a joke over the way that I have avoided direct answers to many of her questions.)

P-3   "Well, I know that I have lived a very sinful life. I guess I have chalked up a score of something like fifteen men." (Some suggestion of achievement!)

(She then proceeded to relate frequent relations with a man who was correspondent in her divorce and the perversion that was also involved. This she got out with the greatest difficulty.)

The recounting led to a renewed experience of her current dilemma, guilt, isolation, extensive hospitalization, and frustration in psychotherapy over which she cried a great deal. The occasion for the tears she linked to her morals and her perception that everyone knew about her behavior and condemned her. She owned that there were other strong feelings that troubled her, like anger toward her mother. "I didn't get along very well with Mother. I didn't get along very well with anybody for that matter. One day she said to me:

67

'Why don't you just curse God and die?' So I did. I wasn't really angry with him, but I was with everybody else." She wanted to know if this could be forgiven.

It was all exceedingly painful, and having attempted to offer some assurance, I added: "I have an idea there is more to come." After a struggle, she said: "There is." Then after a long silence in which her distress was manifest, I acknowledged my awareness of her discomfort. She then said that she had talked a good deal already and that the rest she would keep for another time. Upon my initiative, and with her consent, I offered a prayer.

I don't know what values accrued from my efforts to take Mrs. Jones back over experiences she was inclined to pass over because of their pain. She complied with my request. The difficulty she experienced in doing so was very apparent. My interest was based on the theory that the recounting of them might have significant emotional import by way of reexperiencing those same events and evaluating them in the light of subsequent understandings, unmistakable evidence that I had been reading Sigmund Freud and Harry Stack Sullivan.

I was learning how to assist her in dealing with very painful material. When silence ensued I bided my time, then summarized recent sharing. I was still resistive to her questions, choosing to turn them back to her, or alternately, making some oblique response. My reassurance seems to have been based on the belief that statements from me were OK, provided the timing seemed right. I was feeling more freedom to declare myself, to state my views, and at the same time I retained the belief that experience of forgiveness, or acceptance, was superior to any articulation or pronouncement concerning them. I was disappointed that I had to spell out my perceptions, preferring to think that my actions would make the answer unnecessary. I knew Christan concepts, in themselves, had not saved her and that it was through concepts that she was still trying to appropriate her salvation. So reluctantly, with real misgivings, I provided an intellectual interpretation for that which I hoped was already real for her. Perhaps it was. I had my doubts, and by her nonverbal evidences of inner turmoil I was sure that she was far from at peace. I was able, however, to honor her desire to pursue the matter another time.

The projected case conference was at hand. The next time we met I reviewed arrangements and she spoke with more confidence as she felt her relationship with me was continuing to be very helpful. That out of the way, she started relating an account of a period of despondency during which she attempted to take her own life by means of an overdose of sleeping pills. She related to me some of the thoughts she had had as she lay waiting for the pills to take effect, then of her desperate desire for deliverance from them once they began to act upon her. She called on God to help her and she felt he had. She felt subsequently that God had not failed her but that she had failed him. We were back to her sexual dilemmas. This time she felt that her confession was complete and that she would have no more occasion to concern herself with sex. I was not content to let the matter rest.

C-1   "I'm wondering how you see me? You have referred to me as 'a man of the cloth' or 'a man of God,' how else do you see me?"

P-1   "Well, (after a pause) I see you as a good man and as a minister. Ministers for me are always on a pedestal." (She was reminded of her feelings toward men with whom she had had sex relations and expressed wonder at the hatred she experienced. Men were degraded in her eyes and not herself. She reported that another girl had told her this was her feeling too, and a way to express her hatred for men. The patient admitted that there could be some of this in her actions too.)

C-2   "You do see me as a man. Would you be alarmed if you thought that I had sexual feelings?"

P-2 "Well, I think it's right and beautiful inside marriage, but yes, I would be alarmed if I thought that you favored anything else. Do you think sexual relations outside marriage is sinful?"

C-3 "Now, wait a minute! Did I say anything about sex relations? I said sexual feelings."

P-3 "Well, I don't see you as a possible sexual partner, if that is what you mean."

C-4 "I was trying to suggest the importance of recognizing the facts in any relationship. It's good to be open and frank. May I say that I see you, not as a man nor as an asexual person such as you talked about the other day, but as a woman."

The conversation continued in this vein. As Mrs. Jones reflected on her history and her experience of therapy, the chaplain picking up one of her analogies to wonder whether she was trying to use religion "to keep the lid on" while ignoring other means of dealing with her sexuality.

The initiative was with me, and the patient responded happily. My directness may have come from the new awareness on my part that problems in relationships can best be worked out not "out there" but in the context of the relationship being experienced at the moment, the relationship in this case being with me. Asking her how she perceived me, I was ready to tell her how I perceived her and that I had difficulty with her desire to dismiss sex as a continuing problem. I indicated that I would like to continue the subject under discussion another time. I also indicated quite clearly, in the guise of a suggestion, that I wasn't too happy about the direction of some of the conversation, being more at home with religious themes than with the significance of childhood experiences. It would seem that when such references lacked specific religious content, I was less than comfortable and made efforts to return to the present. I felt there might well be therapeutic potential there, but my interest in staying with her at that level had diminished with the passage of time.

Religious content or current relationships I felt more secure about, both from the standpoint of competence and avoidance of trespass on the domain of psychiatrist or psychologist, which I was not. Was I justified in this or unduly sensitive? Was her sharing of sensitivities about her past something that I should have been ready to receive simply because she wanted to share them? Hesitant in that direction, I displayed a new boldness in the other. I was bold in focusing on our perception of each other as male and female. I was not free from anxiety, for I hastened to correct her impressions lest she misunderstand my intentions. It was all in good humor and our friendship remained strong.

Mrs. Jones greeted me some days later with genuine excitement. She had used our conversation on the previous occasion with reference to her femininity. When talking subsequently with her doctor, he had confirmed that she was progressing and that was good news. Yes, "and the doctor says that he sees me as a woman, that I'm not away out in left field." Obviously, she felt affirmed. I didn't pause to celebrate with her. I pursued another agenda.

C-4 "You told me the other day something about growing up with your brother, but you have said very little about your father. What kind of a person was he?"

P-5 "He wasn't a very strong character. He and mother quarreled a lot, but mother usually had her way. He was very severe. He didn't beat me more than once or twice when I was quite small, but he was very severe on the boys. They were afraid of him."

C-5 "I take it that you didn't feel very close to him."

P-6 "No, not really. He used to play a lot with us when we were little, so I'm told. He seemed to like little children. In a way I think he was more capable of affection than my mother."

C-6 "He wasn't a strong character but there was something about him that you could appreciate. (Pause) I mentioned your father because it has been

71

said that some people have trouble in thinking about God if they have an unhappy experience of their own father. You know God is often referred to as Father, as a male person."

P-7   "I know. He is the only man that hasn't let me down . . . until you came along."

C-7   "I was reading your chart the other day in preparation for the case conference, and I noticed that at one time you had the idea that God told you not to eat."

P-10   "Don't you believe that God can tell a person to fast?"

C-10   "Frankly, I don't know. I have never had such an experience myself. If God asked you to fast, what do you suppose his purpose would be?"

Here was an instance where I invited some reporting from the past. "What was her father like?" (C-4). A concise and fairly comprehensive statement was offered, whereupon I introduced a religious concept. The first thing I knew she had taken us out of the past and into the present, away from the conceptual and into the personal (P-7). I was willing to be personal only up to a point. Previously I had invited it, but here I wasn't prepared to face it. Whatever the reason for my reticence, my own agenda or anxiety, I passed by the opportunity to take a look at her feelings toward me. I diverted the conversation to her previously reported experience of God telling her not to eat. She showed no embarrassment in talking about this part of her history though she knew that others had considered it strange. It was still real to her, and I treated it as real (C-9, 11). At least I did not show surprise or disbelief. I asked her to confirm that she had no doubts about its nature, and I asked her to speculate as to the purpose that God might have had in giving such instruction. (Recently I had read of Anton Boisen, a pioneer in CPE, who himself had had hallucinations during an illness and who in his later book, *Exploration of the Inner World,* maintained that all such symptoms have a profound meaning for the patient and are purposeful if we can just discover the meaning.[2]) She had an answer which I found, personally, to be less than satisfactory. I did not tell her so but proffered another scripture reference which in my indirect way I hoped would lead her to further question the meaning of her auditory experience.

The two of us had come through about two months of meeting together which had been spent in getting acquainted, and with confession of one sort or another being a prominent feature. Now it seemed that phase was about over. We had each come to that conclusion. Yet when we sat down together again, Mrs. Jones indicated that there were still further sins she wanted to tell me about.

Two different preoccupations emerged as continuing concerns; consulting fortunetellers and recurring sexual fantasies. I now assess my response to the former as teaching—discerning the spirits to see if they be of God. To the latter, I came perilously close to saying that because it was a common occurrence with others, she didn't need to worry about it. Both the experience of "voices" and of sexual fantasies were sensitive topics, the occasion for ridicule or dispute in the past, not easily shared—and now they were out in the open without blame.

The next meeting began with celebration. Thanksgiving Day had come and gone. Mrs. Jones had visited relatives and come away with a new appreciation of them. Her mood was buoyant. She recalled a movie about Noah and his three sons and couldn't say why it had come to mind. When I offered the theory that she was experiencing a new surge of life even as Noah did in the movie, she gave a tentative assent. "I have not thought of that, but it could be. (pause) I seem to experience people differently, my aunt and uncle for instance, and even the feeling I have about people talking about me. I'm not so sure that they are any more."

With this she recounted other instances where her previous interpretations of her experience were being called into question, in the course of which more history was shared and I tried to associate the new perspectives with the experience of forgiveness. She seemed to accept this without wishing to pursue it. She concluded: "Anyway, I know I feel a whole lot better."

There was no mistaking the direction in which she was moving. No doubt previous psychotherapeutic efforts, like the new response to medication, were bearing fruit.

The process continued. A few days later Mrs. Jones reported that she now had a different understanding of her earlier refusal to eat. She now felt, she said, that it was related to her feelings that people were talking about her and out to harm her; might even put poison in her food. Since she now questioned the reality of this, she seemed to feel that she would no longer be faced with this kind of experience again.

She went on to tell me something else she had shared with her doctors but from which as yet she had experienced no relief. She related in some detail about one of her brothers and about the low esteem in which the family as a whole had been held by the community.

C-8   "I wonder why you feel it is important to tell me all about your brother and about the emotional difficulties of others in your family?"

P-8   (After some hesitation) "I just feel that I told you those other things and I felt better. And these things have bothered me a great deal for years and years. I would like to feel better about them."

C-9   "I still don't see how you think this might help."

P-9   "Also, as my therapist, I thought it might help you to understand. There might be some things that it would be important for you to know."

C-10   "I don't know that I can accept the title which you have given me, but I can say that it does give me a more complete picture of you. But I wonder if you might also have been doing one of two things. Could you have been trying to justify or explain why you are the way you are?"

P-10   (With a bit of agreement) "Well, no, I don't think so. I know that I have been responsible for many of my actions."

C-11   "Or could you have been inviting an opinion, as if you have some doubt about there being any hope for you, your past being what it is?"

P-11   "Well, maybe, but I've never got the impression from the doctors that I am hopeless. They have encouraged me to go out and to look for a job at different times. I don't think I'm hopeless. I don't know—maybe I am."

C-12   "Let me tell you what I think about that. I don't think that you are hopeless. I believe that you have made progress, and that you can make a great deal more. I have an idea though that you may need to discover or recover more of a sense of purpose than you have shared with me. Have you had a sense of purpose this far in life?"

This invitation to relate her vocational history seems abruptly to have cut across the flow of her interest. I have no complete answer for my abruptness, verging on rejection of that which I had been accepting for some time. I do know that I had been reading and was involved in discussions of Victor Frankl's work and its emphasis on current meanings and purpose in living now and consequently the downgrading of past history in the treatment process.[3] That emphasis appealed to me, as it has done to many ministers, because it seems to be less ambiguously an appropriate focus for pastoral concern. I was further discomfitted by her designation of me as her therapist, for to depart from the role of the pastor was, as I then perceived the attitudes and emphases of my training program, a no-no. In my enthusiasm, I related my hopes for her through discovery of a purpose for living. I invited her (which had the effect of direction) to give a history of her vocational quest. Would Frankl have been interested in her vocational past? Somehow I don't think so.

If my heavy-handedness had any negative impact, it was

not apparent in the sessions that followed. Mrs. Jones quickly resumed her account of difficulties with her brother, mingled with difficulties in relating to other people, both past and present.

P-5　"One of my problems is that I don't get along with people too well (glancing uneasily about the ward). I don't have much to do with other patients and some of them think I'm stuck up. I know that I am often preoccupied. I appear to be looking at them, but I don't see them."

With that we quickly returned to history in which her shame over sexual activity led to habitual avoidance of eye contact. I had not been aware of this in her relating to me, and this she explained as due to her trust in me. Her struggle for self-esteem as a youth was recounted, her ugly duckling appearance, her pride in her morals, the strictness of her mother, her mother's high standards.

What did this review of history accomplish? It did enlarge my understanding of her past. It may be that I became more understanding of her. It highlighted a paradox in her life. To that extent it may have been useful, for she had another occasion to reflect on the conflict she had experienced within herself and the sources of some of those values to which she continued to cling, in spite of the fact that she did reject some parts of her inherited standards. It pointed to the nature of her struggle, to use what was valid from her past without being bound to that which did not serve her. She said the conversation was useful. I interpreted her remark as showing that her desire for conversation was at an end. She did not move to leave however, so I sat in silence. The initiative was hers.

P-23　"I have another problem. I find it very difficult to talk with people. I make some people think that I don't want to talk to them because I think I'm better than they are. If they only knew! It's the very opposite to the way I feel! I feel very inferior for many reasons as I have told you, and I am very conscious of how much of a sinner I am."

C-23 "It seems people don't understand."

P-24 "If they only knew how I have felt all these years, struggling with all these things by myself, wanting to tell someone but not being able to."

C-24 "You feel your mother wouldn't understand."

P-28 "I used to think that people could read my mind. I don't really think that anymore but I still don't like to expose myself."

C-28 "Did you feel this way on your recent visit?"

P-29 "No, but I still feel that way around here."

C-29 "You feel this is something you would like to overcome?"

I can't help but wonder how the conversation would have gone if I had been able to catch the nowness of P-24. Why I chose to hark back to her experience of her mother I cannot say. I can see how that led her to think of her exhusband who couldn't understand, and then by contrast to me. The patient completed the circle. The end result may have been the same in terms of content, but something of subtle feeling tone was lost I think. It lacked the gratitude, the appreciation, the outright statement of celebration of the original. I acknowledged then the personal reference, but in so doing I exercised control of the conversation, taking the focus away from me, in favor of a general question to which she responded. From her standpoint the need for change was still real. How she viewed the possibility for change was not recognized by me at this time and was not explored.

Sometimes interviews were difficult to reconstruct in verbatim form. Hence in the interests of an overall picture of the relationship between us, a synoptic report was used from time to time. What follows is the outline of the session on December 8.

The patient began the conversation with an enthusiastic report that previous conversations, in particular the last, were bearing fruit. She said she was recalling feelings that she had long since forgotten concerning her first infatuation and related sexual activity, feelings of guilt, anxiety, and fear.

The chaplain wondered just how the reliving of these old feelings helped her as she said it did. Her reply was to the effect that she understood herself better, and other people too. When asked if this made it easier for her to get along with people on the ward, she indicated that her relations on the ward were still the same, because she didn't like smalltalk.

When the chaplain asked if she knew why this might be so, she reported that many feelings had been coming back to her during recent days, and she was realizing more and more how resentment and hostility toward others had shaped her activities from her teens. She thought her withdrawal from others started back there. Psychiatrists in months of psychotherapy had tried to tell her this but she wouldn't accept it at that time. Only now was she able to admit responsibility for her own isolation. The chaplain led her back over this material the second time, then asked how this new awareness of responsibility for relationsips made her feel. Her reply was that she hardly knew where to begin.

This cast her relationship with God into a new light. Her concern could now be directed elsewhere, to reconstruction (her word), but she confessed to not having a clue as to how.

The chaplain explained his understanding of his role as encouraging and supporting her in her efforts to resume responsibility for herself. She indicated that this was the same attitude as the doctors'; that all they could do was help her to help herself.

As I read the notes, I could sense her enthusiasm for what was happening. I'm sure I shared her excitement and satisfaction to a point, but I couldn't get too excited unless the insights were actually being translated into action. Hence the gentle yet persistent search for explanations of current blocks, and some tendency to lift up parts of my reality as a test for hers. She continued to elaborate and explore her new perspectives of the past, to acknowledge her own responsibility for much of her trouble in the past, and to recognize how her distortion of reality in the past had included her understanding of the nature of her relationship with God.

There were references to the future, wistful, fleeting, and largely unexamined. Confirmation of the responsibility which now rested with her was good news, and also bad news. Could she respond? Could she rise to the challenge? Could she persevere and cast off her bondage? Anxious to reassure and encourage her, I pointed to her initiatives with me as evidence that she was on her way.

The magnitude of the challenge was every day before her. How could she do what she hadn't been able to do before? The next conversation began with the patient reporting a recent experience. Snatches of our conversation follow.

C-1   "How did you happen to meet this fellow?"

P-1   "A couple of us were having coffee. All the tables were full except for this one, and he was alone. (pause) He seemed very nice. You have made me aware of the fact that I don't know how to talk to people. I have tried, but I just don't know what to say. If they say something to me I can respond, but if they don't have anything to say I am at a loss."

P-7   "I think if I could feel better about myself then maybe I could talk better."

P-10   (After a pause) "Well, I do feel that I'm a better person than I was. I am more aware of other people, more understanding, more tolerant of others . . . This is good, but I still can't take the initiative in talking to people. If they speak first I can respond, but I can't seem to speak up."

C-11   "I'm wondering what it was that I said or did to make you aware, as you said, of this problem?"

P-11   "Well, I find it easy to talk to you, but when you asked me if I had tried talking with others, taking the initiative, I tried and I found I couldn't. I guess I've been shut up too long. I told you about that therapy group at ———— where they wouldn't let me talk. (Chaplain nodded.) And at home I was told for years that I was to be seen and not heard. Dr. ———— told me he thought one of my troubles was that I had isolated myself so long that now it is hard to get away from it."

P-13   "Part of my trouble, too, is the fact that I am only listening part of the time. Mostly, I am in a world of my own. I listen just enough to respond occasionally, but often my thoughts are far away. It's not that I deliberately do this. It's involuntary, I think."

C-17   "You know, I haven't really been aware of this in our conversation together."

P-17   "Oh, that's because I'm interested. I look forward to these sessions. I guess I want to gain absolution or something. I want to be different than I am, and you make me feel that you are interested in my problems."

It was a simple matter now for Mrs. Jones to pinpoint problems. It was something else to deal with them. The chaplain could sometimes recognize and acknowledge understanding of the resultant feelings but was more inclined to pick up and pursue inferences from the content of her sharing, either by means of leading questions (C-11) or by introduction of what seemed like related data (C-17). This last reference is a good illustration of consequence. In P-17 the patient had made a passing reference to absolution. I took that as a clue and embarked on what I now consider a wild goose chase. My quest determined my agenda for the rest of the session. Could I, in her fantasy world, detect a possible source for her continuing feelings of guilt? My efforts may have had some relevance for the patient, but they seem not to have had much of life or of power because she minimized problems in the area touched upon. Her denial of current stress over this question seemed genuine. As I now view my part in this session, it seems to me I had my own ideas about the cause of her inhibitions and guided the conversation into further consideration of guilt rather than of her current fears

80

and excitement, not the least of which was her interest in her conversations with me and the hope which she found therein.

"I don't have very much to talk about today." This was the opening sentence. But with that was a brief report of conversation with her doctor indicating improvement, but not yet readiness for employment. Into the silence that followed Mrs. Jones introduced a topic, shared information, to which I responded by confirming what I understood of the content. Then we were back to silence and the earlier theme of not many problems to talk about. The future concerned her, but she didn't intend to face it until after Christmas. But having said that, she invited me to make suggestions. I asked a question which led her to acknowledge her insecurity except when in familiar territory, i.e., Texas, her home state. Inexplicably, I raised the question of Christmas plans and this maintained the conversation for a time. Then we were back to the earlier theme: "It seems I don't have much to say today." I began to wonder if this was a way of questioning whether we should continue to meet, and I raised this with her.

C-15   "You have said something like that a couple of times today. Does this raise the question as to the need for our continuing to meet together?"

P-16   "I suppose it does. Perhaps we don't need to meet as often." (She related that how at ———— she had met for weeks on end with a therapist and sat in silence as did he. She felt badly about wasting his time, since she did not feel able to talk, and also felt that she would much rather be back doing ceramics, which she would otherwise be doing. She asked if the chaplain had seen that kind of therapy and told something of what she had done.)

C-16   "I gather that sitting in silence really bothered you then. What about now?"

P-17   "Oh, I don't feel threatened by it the way I was then. You seem so relaxed and not in a hurry. Of course, my therapist at ———— said that the time was for me and that I could use it any way I wanted it, but it didn't seem to make sense to just sit there when he was so busy. I don't feel the same way with you, but maybe I don't need as much time."

This excerpt is of more than passing import. The relationship had been maintained at a consistent level for almost three months despite the prognostications of the doctor. Was his prediction about to come true? There seemed to be little anxiety by me in the face of this possibility. My evaluation at that time included discussion of the impact of this realization. I concluded that I could recognize that some disappointment was there. Mrs. Jones carried most of the conversation. It had a free and easy quality to it, apart from the recurrent reporting of "It seems I don't have much to say today." She seemed readily to agree that less time might be indicated. "I suppose it does" (P-16) suggests some ambivalence perhaps. She did lay claim to some time in the immediate future. She did not want to be cut off entirely (C-17). The verbatim noted the buoyancy of the patient. Was there any threat for her in the possible fading of our relationship? I recorded that I did not experience the silence during the early part of the session as raising the possibility of termination and toward the end did not experience it as a threatening possibility, though I am sure that subconsciously there was a sense of possible disappointment. I now wonder whether Mrs. Jones experienced my reference to the possibility of termination as a threat to her increased sense of security and well-being.

Three days later this is how the conversation began:

P-1　"I really don't have anything to talk about today."
C-1　"Nothing seems very pressing."

P-2　"That may seem a bit strange, but that's the way it is." (She didn't seem in the least bit disturbed about this.)

C-2   "That's fine. We can sit here and chatter and if nothing develops we can call it quits until another time." (A couple of minutes of silence followed.)

P-3   "Say, I have a question I want to ask you. Do you believe that it is wrong to be divorced and remarried?"

C-3   (With emphasis and a smile) "Well, that is a question."

P-4   (Laughs heartily)

C-4   "And you would like a simple straightforward answer? (jokingly)."

P-5   (Laughing) "Yes."

C-5   "What do you think about it?"

Drawing her out, sharing my biblical knowledge and my convictions and my difficulties with any legalistic solution to the problem, we had a spirited interchange in which it became clear that she was rethinking her views about divorce, with the possibility of remarriage in the back of her mind.

Christmas brought a brief interlude and some new experiences which were shared when next we met. Mrs. Jones had called her exhusband and had discovered that he was now divorced for the third time. She was reevaluating her image of him, concluding that he was not as understanding or considerate of others as she had tended to assume. We soon ran into a silence again.

Again the silence was broken by the patient's asking for an explanation of the New Covenant. I used that to question her again about her conception of God and to discuss the meaning of forgiveness.

Mrs. Jones was insistent upon God's judgment as meaning: "We always pay for the wrong we do."

C-12   "Are you saying that he is always faithful in his judgment?"

P-12   "He's faithful and he forgives, but we still have to pay."

C-13   "Am I saying the same thing, I wonder? He forgives us, but the scars remain."

P-13   "That's it, exactly. The scars remain."

C-14   "There is something else which must be said though. That illustration doesn't apply as well to human relationships. One person may wrong another person and may be forgiven, and in a sense things are never the same again because the memory of the wrong may remain, but it may be that the relationship between the two may be better after than it was before."

P-14   "I think that may be very true in my case. Before I was not as tolerant of other people, or as understanding. I am more conscious now of the feelings of other people. And I feel more peace than I have for years. I guess that is all that we can expect in this life. I mean that we can never know complete security. There will always be insecurity in this life."

C-16   (Pause) "I certainly agree with what you say but somehow you give me an uncomfortable feeling when you say it . . . I'm not sure just why that is but maybe because I feel that you have the idea that you can't expect to experience anything much different than what you experience right now."

P-16   "That is how I feel (with feeling). That's a true insight."

C-17   "If that is the way you feel I would hope that you could come to feel something different about yourself, but I am not sure at this point just what I can do to help you. (pause) Perhaps I could make a personal witness . . . I believe that I am a sinner, a forgiven sinner, but more than that I believe that God has given me talents or abilities which are worthwhile, and that he will enable me to do things that are worthwhile if only I can keep my life open to him. I don't have all the answers. Often I feel uncertain as to whether or not I have what it takes to do some of the things which seem to be opportunities, but I try, believing that if I am willing God can use whatever abiltities I have for good. (pause) I am not sure how all this applies to you, but I think that your attitude to yourself, and my attitude to myself, have a lot in common. Perhaps you can tell me what the difference is."

P-17   (With hesitation) "Well, I would say that it is the magnitude of my sin."

C-18   "I have the feeling that when you say that you are thinking primarily of your sexual offenses."

P-18   "Yes. My sin is much worse than yours."

C-19   "I can't buy that. I may not have done what you have done, but I believe that other sins which may not be as obvious may be just as serious. I think you said a little while ago that it is what is inside which really counts."

Here we have an intellectual exchange, not without some emotional overtones, essentially dealing with the content of religious concepts and beliefs. There was scant attention given in the record to the emotional dimension which contained two elements: some celebration of her improvement and also a resignation to her present level of functioning. The latter exercised me (C-16). I wasn't able to accept her doubts about her future. In effect, I protested her attitude which to me smacked of feelings of uselessness. When she, with strongness of affect, affirmed the accuracy of my perception of her thinking about herself and her future, I was even more perplexed and troubled (C-18). I had admitted my uncertainty and impotence to change what she experienced, but I registered my protest anyway. I invited her response by using a directed question. Neither formal doctrine nor personal witness did anything but confirm her view of her own helplessness. The disagreement between us was not heated or sharp, but it was real. Rather than face it, I offered what now seems like a pious platitude and a specious hope.

IV

What Has Gone Wrong? Help!

The title suggests that there was an immediate awareness of trouble ahead. That is not so. It was the end of the year. The relationship seemed to have changed since confession was no longer called for. The repentance, the desire for change was real, and the responsibility for it rested heavily upon an oft-defeated person, a patient, and a would-be believer. Nevertheless, the relationship appeared to be intact and the relevance of the Christian faith, which I represented on the ward and to the patient, seemed to be as true as ever. She had her problem of how to change, and I had my earnest and increasingly strong, if not desperate, desire and need to help. That statement calls for some background. Remember the magnitude of the undertaking I had assumed? With a large family and scant financial resources, I and my family had been adjusting to the complex demands of a new setting. Resources were dwindling as the anticipated parttime employment of my wife was slow to materialize.

I was one of a class of twelve, many of them recent graduates of large American seminaries. There were rigorous academic demands in the program along with the clinical assignments. My assignment in a seminar on "The Psychiatric View of Man" was Freud's concept of illness and health. To my dismay, I soon found that I had to read through much of Freud in order to pick up the many scattered references to the subject. My resulting paper was rated by the professor as of excellent quality as to the content, but the presentation of it to the class was weak. Concurrently, I was spending twenty hours a week in the hospital, writing three verbatims a week for my chaplain supervisor, participating weekly in an interpersonal relations group, and assorted conferences and seminars.

In mid-November there was a routine midterm evaluation, a conference between myself and two supervisors. Its purpose was to assess progress and the appropriateness of the goals which I had in mind. I knew that I was not making the progress I wanted to make. I didn't know what the obstacles really were. I experienced the problem largely in terms of not really being able to please the supervisor, sensing that while I was meeting some positive and even exciting results on the ward, I really wasn't on top of what was happening, not really knowing what or why, and therefore not in any sense in command of myself or of my situation. The message I took from the evaluation was, in effect, "unless there is some major breakthrough, your goals seem unrealistic. You are too restricted. You need to become more free if you are to achieve your ambition."

The message was received without protest and without demand. I felt clueless as to how to proceed. How does one become more free? It was very much like the question of my patient: "How can I change?" You may well ask why this personal dilemma of mine was not shared with Mrs. Jones. I can see now that this would have been a much more personal way of sharing than what I had attempted at the end of the year. There may be several reasons why it didn't happen. It did not occur to me. That may suggest two things about me at the time, both pointing to lack of flexibility or freedom. I now conclude that I was firmly wedded to the idea that the patient's past must be the locale of her current difficulties, that her personal experience of guilt and shame and worthlessness could mean that she had not yet experienced the unconditional love of God. That sustained me in my interest and efforts to make that love known and available to her. The other indicator of my proscribed position is the knowledge that I was then more comfortable in reporting personal history than in sharing current personal struggles. I further struggled with the impression that in good counseling neither personal history nor personal problems had any place.

The parallel between the two of us was even more striking than has just been indicated, though I didn't recognize it at the time. My personal dilemma continued to build. Soon it was expressed in a physical symptom. My digestion began to bother me. It wasn't severe but it was persistent. The warning was clear. I was experiencing stress, and I understood that stress could lead to ulcers. Weren't there textbooks on psychosomatic illnesses, ulcers being one of them? I resolved to seek psychotherapy for the twofold purpose of resolving the problem of stress and of seeking a larger freedom in my functioning. This last purpose is a common occcurrence among would-be therapists and counselors, therapy in pursuit of professional goals.

Before that was instituted there was further data which surfaced worthy of consideration. There was the annual pastor's course in which trainees like myself were commonly used as resource personnel in small groups made up of pastors. My participation in that group, I was told, was very different from my performance in a group of my peers. Was it the same person who spoke with confidence and apparent strength in the one context and not in the other? What did my peers do to me? Or was it something I did to myself. What and why? The same phenomenon seemed to be operative in my conduct of a worship service in the presence of faculty and a group of my peers. My material was very acceptable, so I was told, but I appeared to be tense, my voice noticeably higher than under normal circumstances.

My psychotherapist, a psychiatrist, though not a psychoanalyst, was very much interested in my history. He took me through my past from early childhood memories to experiences of my youth and young adulthood. As I talked I became aware of a persistent theme. I seemed very competitive. Whether in school or in sports or in other relationships I seemed prone to compare myself with others. I was up or I was down. During my childhood I had been a good student and a good athlete. I had won recognition. The move to the big city at age fifteen had changed all that. I was scarcely noticed in school though my grades were credible. The sports in which I had excelled were not played in the city, and city sports were completely strange to me. I was younger than most of my classmates, less experienced in the ways of the world, and had no money to assist my participation in the larger life of my new environment.

I could see how the habitual comparison with others had continued through the years. I would make the "college try." I would often function well but seldom with lasting satisfaction. Even when there was no apparent competition, I would invariably feel that my performance could have been, and therefore should have been, better. When I was very much aware of the demand or competition, I was anxious and less than my best. It was all laid out so clearly as I related my life experience to the doctor. He didn't ask many questions. He didn't make many comments, I did most of that for myself as I went along. He said just enough to let me know that he was getting the picture and, at times, that there were some areas that had not been touched upon. He was soft-spoken, gentle, respectful and, I felt, caring. With his guidance and support I was looking at my present difficulties against the background of my past. I was coming to some appreciation of the origin of my fearful comparison of myself with others, a strong tendency to minimize my gifts and to feel insecure whenever there was in my unconscious the likelihood of an unfavorable comparison.

I had seen it in Mrs. Jones. In fact, she had said it. Part of her growing understanding of herself was that she had for years been preoccupied with the judgments of those around her, whereas she had assumed that her problems with guilt and failure were in relation to the judgment of God. She had come to perceive that this was true of her some weeks before I had any awareness of the truth of my bondage to similar fears, not of God, but of my fellow humans.

When I did come to realize what I had been doing to myself by this means, I could see how inappropriate it was, how groundless, and how self-defeating. I had two authorities for coming to such a conclusion. The most immediate was the psychiatrist. Not that he told me so, but I sensed his support for my own view that this habitual pattern could be and should be broken. The other aid to evaluating this behavior was my Christian heritage. Was my worth dependent on the judgment of my fellow human beings or was it dependent on the judgment of God? Obviously, the latter was the answer of the faith I professed. Moreover, God's judgment, I believed, was tempered by the knowledge of the gifts he had bestowed on me as a unique being and, further, that the value placed on me was not conditional upon my faithfulness in stewardship. His mercy and his love, so I professed to believe, was stronger than any failure or any sin on my part. So why be anxious in the presence of one's peers? Why be afraid of making a mistake? Why fear failure? Why, indeed!

I now had a new awareness of myself. I now had a clearer understanding of what my professed faith should deliver me from. I set about the conscious task of living daily out of that faith, of setting aside the temptation to make comparisons, of risking mistakes, and of accepting the possibility of failure. My digestive symptoms disappeared.

Meanwhile, concurrent with my attempts to deal responsibly with my own needs as just described, I also moved to grapple with my need for a better understanding of the counseling process. I had come with many vague impressions of do's and don'ts. I had read books of repute most of which I allowed to inhibit me, to laden me with idealistic goals of competence which enhanced the possibilities of the failure I so much disliked. I had wrestled with Freud and had some sense of the structure in which he and subsequent psychoanalysts functioned, but I wasn't a psychoanalyst. I had studied the methods of Harry Stack Sullivan with some thoroughness, but again, I wasn't a psychiatrist. Throughout the fall I had been exposed to a number of psychiatric theories and techniques, but none had taken hold of me or struck me as particularly adaptable to me as a minister. My lack of a thought-out approach and related skills showed up in all my pastoral relationships, including that with Mrs. Jones. How could I do better?

My quest led me again to the reading list and then to the library where I pulled from the shelf an early book of Carl Rogers, *Counseling and Psychotherapy.*[1] He talked about the vital link of feelings running through all human behavior. Back and beyond the content of words is the dynamic realm of emotion. To help people in distress, it is often the unconscious influence and power of emotions which the therapist must understand and help the client to recognize and use. I had some inkling of such concepts but no appreciation of their power when applied. Nor had I anything but a very hit-and-miss track record in my attempts to recognize and stay with the feelings of my patients when I did attempt to do so.

The ward provided a dramatic instance of this just at that time. An older Spanish American woman with a history of previous admissions had not responded to any of the various therapies they had tried with her in this hospital stay. She seemed intent to remain incoherent, speaking Spanish if the audience did not understand Spanish, and mumbling so that no one could understand if the audience had command of both Spanish and English. A consulting psychiatrist was asked to see her and the usual incoherent mumble was displayed. The consultant began putting into words the feelings he identified and before long she was speaking to him in limited fashion, but nonetheless coherently. What a challenge to go out and do likewise!

What made Rogers' book the more helpful was that in the back of the book there was page after page where extracts from a counseling session were set out. The reader was invited to cover the counselor's responses, to make an independent attempt to phrase the feelings expressed, and then to compare responses with that of the counselor. Laboriously, I worked my way through its pages. Why was my response so different? Gradually, I caught on. The counselor asked no questions. He made no comments. His responses were accurate reflections of the other's communication, not a repetition of the content but a recognition of the message conveyed by the words. Sometimes the significance of many words could be caught in a single word, and often detailed recounting would be encapsulated in a single sentence. When the person knew that the counselor understood, then the owner of the experience and of the problem could readily continue on with the search for self-understanding or problem resolution. I wanted to be able to counsel like that. I now had a model which I thought I could use.

That isn't where I started the New Year with Mrs. Jones, however. She was available, as usual, to meet with me. She had a cold and signs that she was suffering from it. She was not noticeably down in spirit. She took initiatives in the conversation, and she responded to questions from me. Most of these were attempts to have her elaborate on statements previously made. Most were nonevaluative, expressed no opinion, and implied none. This statement does appear in the record nonetheless: "It seems to me that your thinking on this point is pretty mature." If I could pronounce such judgments, why did I later refuse to express any opinion when on another topic she asked for one? What might I be withholding? I don't know whether my inconsistency in this respect registered with her or troubled her in any way. It didn't show. It was apparent that she was wanting to be discharged and was afraid she might not make it on the outside. She was looking for something helpful from me. The best I was able to come up with, knowing that she had had some previous short-lived discharges, was to ask her to compare herself with similar occasions in the past when she had been released. She continued to talk as if discharge was imminent.

When a silence came, marked by mounting tension on the part of Mrs. Jones, I changed the subject to a recent report by another patient expressing appreciation for the way in which Mrs. Jones put herself out for other patients, setting their hair and giving other personal attention. She grinned broadly and said she enjoyed doing things for others, especially when appreciation was expressed. Right away this brought to mind how reluctant she had often been to help her mother and how resentful she had at times become. The contrast with her experience of her mother was pronounced, a comparison which the chaplain encouraged her to pursue, using the occasion to affirm the validity of resisting the unreasonable demands and expectations of others. He equated obligation to slavery and choice to freedom from bondage. She seemed to understand and approve.

In a gentle and permissive but very direct way, I invited an explanation of what she had shared and that led into history. I chose to focus on mention of her mother rather than to recognize the good feelings stemming from appreciation. The move did give another and different glimpse of her past, and another perspective of her needs and vulnerability in that moment. My speeches, as they appear to me now, reported my personal discomfort and implied that I was in a position to affirm the importance of the matter in hand, and that I hoped my opinion would carry some weight. At the time I had no inclination to question the validity of what I had done.

Next time Mrs. Jones carried the conversation initially with inquiries about my studies and the health of my family. She appeared quite eager, but silence soon came. Noting her signs of agitation, but not commenting on them, I accepted responsibility for a new agenda. Relating an anecdote from my recent reading, I declared my desire to heed the words of the person in the story who told his minister that words of assurance about his future were less important to him than the assurance that, in success or failure, the minister would not forsake him. Her response was in terms of the security some of her Catholic friends found in the church, and the risks and uncertainty of finding any such security herself.

The choice of subject matter here seemed to flow naturally from her previous preoccupation with discharge and the risk of failure attendant thereto. The anecdote brought an animated response. Mrs. Jones put it in an ecclesiastical and personal context which implied her own ambivalence about standards and her fear of the consequences of failure. She had her own way of dealing with the risk of rejection, avoidance of a community that might reject her, the church. Met with challenge, she listened attentively to suggestions of personal responsibility, and responded with alacrity to my picture of a church which could be an understanding and accepting community. Evaluative comment on the verbatim at that time pointed to the longer speeches of both parties as indicative of a great freedom on both sides. Was it really so?

There were signs that all was not well with the patient. The heavy cold persisted. She slept a good deal during the daytime. She missed an appointment with me once. A few days later, roused from sleep for medication, she sat down with me looking very sleepy and reported that she had been asleep for two hours. I have tried to capture the gist of the conversation:

P-2   "I guess I'll be staying here for a while. Dr. ———— says they don't discharge patients, women patients especially, until they have some definite plan. I don't have any right now."

C-3   "That leaves it pretty much up to you, doesn't it?"

P-3   "I don't know about Dr. ————. I didn't say anything to him. (pause) I guess I'll just have to stay here and grow fat (with laughter). Do you know, I have gained over twenty pounds in the last couple of months!"

C-7   "How do you account for it?"

P-7   "I guess I'm not as tense as I used to be, and I get more benefit from the food I eat. I believe it has something to do with metabolism (her word)."

P-12   "I don't have delusions much any more, and when I do it doesn't bother me the way it used to."

C-13   "How come?"

P-13   "Well, if people are talking about me . . . I don't think they are very much . . . I just don't care. That's what they tried to teach us at ————. It's a sign of maturity not to pay any attention."

A long silence intervened during which glances were exchanged several times. Finally, with a smile, I said:

C-15   "That's about the longest silence we've had. How do you feel about it?"

P-15   "Alright. Of course, there have been many times when I have been fearful of silence."

C-17   "I was responding to this, I think, for you had said something like this before when I was concerned to know whether you experienced the silence as a threat."

P-7   "Not with you. (pause) There are times, too, with other people when I just become lost in my own thoughts, to the point where I can actually forget they are there, and many times of course I just follow what is being said closely enough to respond once in a while, but I'm not really there."

C-18   "How do you suppose it is that you experience me different from other men you have been with?"

P-18   "I think it is because you are so relaxed."

C-19   "I don't understand that, because actually I get a bit uneasy sometimes as I have mentioned. But still you don't seem to feel threatened."

P-19   "No."

Despite the evidence of relapse and the disappointment reported that day, Mrs. Jones retained her sense of humor. Her swing from gravity to laughter, which had a frivolity and lightness about it, was very noticeable and had a genuine ring. It was a strange combination of embarrassment and pleasure so far as I could tell. There was no awkwardness or impatience on her part. There was a willing compliance to volunteer more of her feelings and thoughts concerning her weight gain.

Questions continued to be characteristic of my participation, questions closely related to the patient's offerings, intended to assist her in continued exploration of the many sides of her experience. "Why" was a common directive to which she usually gave some limited explanation, but more reflective statements also met with the same kind of response. Closer examination leads me to the conclusion that reflection of content rather than feelings lacks the dynamism of recognized emotional expression. Hence, breaks in the flow of conversation were frequent, punctuated by recurring silences.

Mention has previously been made to occasions when the discomfort of my companion seemed to me to be considerable, as evidenced by the wringing of her hands and the twisting of her mouth. There was none of that following P-13. Observation pointed to the conclusion that she was accepting of the silence. I didn't trust the perception and subsequently felt that I had to explain my intervention. When she made a distinction between her experience with me and with others again, I went hunting for an explanation. This evoked a perception of me which seemed important to her (P-18). That posed another question for me. Was I really that relaxed? My self-perception was otherwise (C-19), but having acknowledged that I recognized the consequence for her, she didn't feel threatened.

The conversation moved finally to the confidence she had once placed in a young man. "I did trust him . . . so much that when I got hurt I decided I would never trust anyone again, and I haven't—not even my husband." From this distance, without the awareness of her deteriorated ward routine, it is difficult to detect signs of deterioration in the conversation. The silences were ambiguous. They could mean withdrawal into her own private world for unhealthy reasons. They could be an evidence of greater relaxation and an increased sense of well-being. I conclude that there was some sense of buoyancy in her presentation of herself, for though I could not reconstruct the sequence afterward, I did propose that we have a prayer of thanksgiving, to which she readily agreed.

The circumstances surrounding our next appointment were similar. She did not appear at the agreed upon time, but did so later in the line-up for medication. She agreed readily when I asked her if she was interested in sitting down to talk. Her sleep pattern became the subject for conversation through my initiative.

Mrs. Jones didn't seem concerned that she was sleeping more during the day. Though she acknowledged that she sometimes wakened early, she declared that her pattern was nothing like that of other girls who were "up and around half the night," evidence of anxiety which she claimed she was not experiencing. Then she thought of one possible source of unrest, her dreams with sexual content. Immediately she dismissed that explanation saying that she knew she could not be held responsible for her dreams. She moved on to express concern about her need to be creative, her doctor's opinion that she was in no condition to leave the hospital, and her fear that further delay would make her reentry into the world more difficult.

I had been speculating in my own mind about possible sources of tension that might explain her changed course and had been conscious of the fact that she had been less available to me except through my initiatives. She always seemed to respond willingly, but why the change? I reported my speculation that she might have some reason for avoiding me. Though I suspected I might be related to her troublesome sexual dreams, she seemed genuinely to have no such association.

This is the background note for the next verbatim record. "In contrast to the previous day, the patient was awake and sitting in the lounge at our usual time of meeting. We adjourned to the visitor's room. She had had a sleep and still looked sleepy, but she talked freely, carrying the conversation for quite some time at a social level. I responded to this, feeling that it was good for her to cultivate conversation at that level. Finally, when there was an interval of silence I spoke up."

C-1   "May I get personal? You look different today."

P-1   "Oh? It must be my hair. I washed it today and Miss ————— set it." (She went on to describe it, said she was going to let her hair grow, that she was tired of the extra work of curling it, and besides it would make her look more dignified.)

C-2   "Dignified?"

P-2   "Yes."

C-3   "How do you mean?"

P-3   "Well, just dignified. I don't know how else to describe it. How do you define dignified?"

C-4   "Oh, I have an idea about that, but I'm really interested in hearing what it means to you."

P-4   "Oh, well, more proper."

C-5   "Is this the way you feel?"

P-5   "It's the way I'd like to feel."

Most of our meetings through these weeks were scheduled, the frequency reduced from earlier months and reduced still further by the occasional times when she did not appear. Once in a while a nonscheduled exchange would take place. Mrs. Jones met me in the hall and proceeded to tell of a dream she had had. It oftens happens in therapy that when the therapist shows interest in dreams, the patient or client will begin to supply them. Now she told the dream in bare outline. It had no meaning whatsoever for me, and she refused to venture any kind of association or meaning which it might have for her. I took her conversation back to an earlier one, the sexual content of her dreams.

C-4   "You feel resentment; you are annoyed. That suggests that you feel pretty strongly about this. Who are you annoyed at?"

P-4   (Laughing) "Nobody. I think it's just my age. Maybe it's the way I'm made. To put it that way though sounds as if I am annoyed at the Lord, because I didn't make myself."

C-8   "A kind of resentment over what is given?"

P-8   "Yes."

C-9   "Well I can share with you in this. There have been times when I wished I were different than I am. I have wished that I didn't have limitations such as I have. I have wanted to be omnipotent, to do things that I can't because I'm the kind of person I am. Sometimes I've had a very hard time accepting reality as I experience it in myself." (Silence)

C-10   "How does it make you feel to hear me speak as I have just now?"

P-10   "I makes me feel that I am not alone, but I don't see what's wrong in being you."

C-11   "You don't?"

P-11   "I mean, you have a high calling; you are married, and you have a family."

C-12   "I hardly know what to say in the face of that. You seem to be saying that I have all that could be desired."

P-12   "Yes, I can't imagine why you would want to be different. (I was tempted to say that I had much to be thankful for.) Of course, I guess no one really knows what another's situation really is. People might say of me, 'she's never had it so good,' and in a way it's true. Everything is done for me. I've got nothing to do or to worry about, but I don't see it that way."

C-13   "I was wondering if you might see that. No one else can really know except from the inside unless feelings are shared, and that means that envy and self-pity are often misplaced."

P-13   "That's right. I had three friends who weren't married when I was, and I had a nice home and a husband and all that. They thought that everything was as it should be, but they didn't know how unhappy I was." (Silence)

Two things are worthy of note here. My patient effectively frustrated me. I experienced it as teasing. She told me the dream. Why? Then she wouldn't talk about it. Why? Was she aware of associations which she did not wish to share? I didn't acknowledge my frustration. Now I ask myself why. I seems so obvious that I was asking her to be transparent, more open, while I myself was refusing to do the same with her. Yet a little later (C-10) I was trying to be more open with my experience of living. There was no response to my confession regarding historic frustrations and struggles to accept my own reality. With a little prodding she first said she couldn't understand, then concluded that no one can know what the feelings of another person may be, judging from outward circumstances only. Was she thinking of herself?

When we met again a few days later, Mrs. Jones had quite a few reflections on previous experiences to report. She had concluded that many of her dreams and delusions reflected a fear of other people. She felt that this was at the back of her difficulties in social relationships also (specifically fear of rejection). I had responded to her by acknowledging some of my sensitivities along these lines. I further contended that fears were often unrealistic and that the only way to have better relationships was to reach out where she could feel some trust in the other person.

Against the background, this exchange is noteworthy. "Today's visit began with questions from the patient regarding the visit of my supervisor. 'Do you still have things to learn?' I explained that I did, having to work on those things about me which might interfere with a helpful ministry. I asked her how she felt, knowing that I had problems to work on too."

P-1   "It makes me feel that I am not like a purple cow. I am not peculiar because I have problems. Does it help you to meet with me?"

C-1   "Yes, it does. I feel that I have learned a good deal from meeting with you."

P-2   "Does it help you to realize that I have problems in relating to people, and it's your problem too?"

C-2   "I'm not sure I understand your question. Are you saying that my problem is the same as yours?"

P-3   "I think you are quite a bit like I am. You are more outgoing, of course, but you are reserved."

After an interval which ended in silence, the conversation took this unexpected turn.

P-17   (With a bit of a grin) "I wish people wouldn't always expect me to be different than I am."

C-17   "This is what you experience?"

P-18   "Yes. They want me to talk more, to be outgoing, to be more like Mrs. ————."

C-18   "You feel they don't accept you as you are?"

P-19   "That's right. I don't know why I should have to be like Mrs. ————. I just want to be myself."

C-19   "I was wondering last time whether you were comparing yourself with her."

P-20   "I think we are a lot alike. She's kind and thoughtful, and she's very religious, but she is more gregarious than I am. In fact, she talks too much. They say that is part of her problem."

C-20   "You say you shouldn't have to be like her?"

P-21   "No, I don't see why I should."

C-21   "Frankly, I don't either. Tell me. Do you feel that I have been pushing you to be different than you are, to be more talkative and outgoing than you are?"

P-22 (A bit timidly) "Yes."

C-22 "I guess you are right. I have been wanting you to reach out and I guess this means that I have been unwilling to accept you just as you are. That's not the way I would want you to feel about me."

P-23 "I think that you haven't really rejected me. What you wanted is what you think is in my best interests."

C-23 "I suppose that may be so, but just the same it shouldn't have happened. (pause) I wonder—are there other areas where you feel I really haven't been accepting you just as you are?"

In view of the importance I have subsequently attached to this meeting, I include in full the evaluation written at the time:

"I have very mixed feelings about this interview. On the one hand, the patient was leading out as in fact I had encouraged her to do. She took the initiative. She was able to tell me how she experienced me. This is good. On the other hand, I was thrown off balance somewhat by her insight and did not know how to respond. I accepted her judgment, then sought to explore something of what this meant in terms of our relationship with each other. Confronting her bore no immediate fruit.

"Again at P-17 the patient took the initative and demonstrated some strength in her protest against those who will not accept her as she is. This was a general charge not directed specifically at me, and when we had looked at it for a time I asked her if she felt I had been pushing her to be different (C-21). Again I felt this was a significant exchange for her, but I did not know how to respond. I pleaded guilty. In the concluding section which is summarized, I feel I did the right thing in trying to help her by creating a situation in which she would experience feeling. I demonstrated verbally and, I trust, otherwise, that I had learned my lesson about not pushing when she could not express any feeling. It was a very dramatic learning experience for me, and I believe for the patient also."

Reading this evaluation some years later, it seems to me that I did justice to her question to me in P-2 and her impression of me in P-3. She had come to the conclusion that we had something in common. She could see differences of course, but she sensed my reserve. More than that, she had found the courage to tell me about that. Her observation deserved more attention than it received. It was worthy of a celebration. I did not recognize the significance of the occasion. Hindsight seems to have made the difference. Then I agreed with the content, was also vaguely uncomfortable, not knowing what to do with it. More important, I had my agenda. It was a convenient escape from the place where her spontaneous initiative had brought us, but it led nowhere. She was ready to talk about herself, but it was to be her agenda.

It was against that background that Mrs. Jones took the initative which led to the dramatic encounter between us. Never in all our time together had I experienced anything so moving. There was no warning, no threat, for she had generalized her protest, and I could have perceived it as directed at others. Though it was mild, it was earnest. I applied it to myself. I felt judged. She confirmed the verdict, and in the very act of confirmation, she reached out to support and comfort me (P-23). Convicted and forgiven at the same time!

V

Hallelujah

Of course, it wasn't hallelujah right away. I knew I had been doing something wrong, and I was repentant. I could think of several reasons why I had wanted Mrs. Jones to change, to get better. Some were plausible and blameless. Others, like wanting to prove that the doctor was wrong and wanting to enhance my own reputation, I could not defend. Some of these motives I shared with her and some I just alluded to. I felt very humble, and I stated that from henceforth I wanted to show acceptance of her. I wanted to respond to her plea to be accepted without the expectation that she should be different. I said that it could be that she would never be well and, if that were to be the case I still wanted to accept her whatever her condition might be.

The importance of being accepted "just as I am" should not have been lost on me. Had I not so recently come to recognize how my own life had been tyrannized by the habit of comparing myself with others, anxious lest I be compared unfavorably and fearing that the judgments of others would coincide with the judgments that I tended to make? Had I not been assisted by a psychiatrist who made no demand that I be different? He supported me in the desire to break the habit, no doubt had the hope that I would, but he gave me no cause to feel that he expected me to break free or that I should. It was enough to know that I had his confidence that I could, if that was what I chose to do.

Moreover, and this was a larger part of my conscious mind,

there was the faith which I professed. My worth, I knew, was not based on what I had accomplished. It wasn't dependent on my compliance to a demand that I change. God's judgment I believed to be real but his love was not conditional. I was rebuilding my new life in the awareness that I had not been living life on that foundation, and that was why I experienced the anxiety, the fear, the restraint, the reserve, the lack of freedom which had been so apparent to others and was increasingly so to me. When I ran into situations where anxiety loomed, I was now telling myself "God accepts me with my limits and with my fears. It doesn't matter so much what the outcome is. His forgiveness is real. What matters if others think less of me?" Of course, such a conviction could do the same for her. My acceptance wasn't necessarily God's acceptance, but I wanted to do what I could to make his acceptance real to her. In that moment, however, I was most conscious of the fact that I had been doing something which she experienced as nonacceptance of her the way she was. She had bestowed on me her gracious forgiveness. I knew I had God's forgiveness. I wanted to do better. I was confident that I could.

In the wake of our meeting, in which Mrs. Jones had confronted me, there were two sessions which I did not report in detail. In the first the topic was dreams. She did not describe them in detail but recognized their frequency and a common theme, fear of other people. She stated that such fears, along with sex, were her two chief problems. I asked if she had any explanation and she replied that she had grown up with fear of father and fear of mother, especially where sex was concerned. In this way, she suggested, her two problems might be related. The other visit, briefer than usual, dealt with the patient's feelings about the changing scene on the ward, especially since two of her companions had been discharged. When conversation lagged, I sought confirmation that there was little felt need to talk. I then moved on to visit with a new patient.

The visit of February 16th was a lengthy one. The

conversation wandered freely but centered around some recent word from her brother and sister-in-law, her own childlessness, her fear of people, and her vagueness of thoughts for the future. She felt the need of further words with her doctor. This led to some discussion of doctors and their ways. The patient quoted with approval a statement of Dr. ———— to the effect that a doctor has to be pretty humble before he can do much for a mental patient. She said not all doctors saw it that way, which was a pity.

I suggested to her that I had not been very humble in my relations with her. I had operated for a long time upon the idea that I could do something for her, and I was determined to do so. Hence I had been pretty aggressive in trying to help her change. I said that I now saw this as wrong, that I couldn't help her on my own, and that I would be most helpful if I didn't try to push but tried primarily to understand.

She responded by saying that perhaps I was harder on myself than I needed to be, because she felt better than she had in years, and she was sure that I had something to do with it. On this note, the session ended.

In the evaluation which followed the verbatim report of this visit, I ended this way: "Reviewing the three sessions since I last wrote an evaluation on this patient, it would seem that she is showing some signs of increasing insight. Her reference to her fears—which become obvious in her dreams and her association with her childhood fears of parents and brothers—would seem to be something new. Her ideas concerning attendance at a school of floral design while living at the hospital would appear to be more realistic than some former ideas. Her weekend pass would also seem to indicate some increased confidence, and her way of relating to me has of late given more indication of personal strength.

"My continuing repentance for earlier aggression appears in the concluding summary portion of the verbatim. It gave her another opportunity to express her feelings toward me and/or what I had done. She ministered to me."

A few days later, I came upon the patient to her surprise.

She jumped, looked startled, and colored a little. We talked about that and again about her fearful dreams. She speculated about the part that medication might have in inducing dreams. She expressed some concern about her sleep patterns and said that she was trying to resist sleep during the day in the interests of sounder sleep at night. My responses were mainly reflective. I did report lack of knowledge where that was appropriate to some of her questions, and I also asked open-ended rather than specific questions. We had to contend with several interruptions. With little sense of her interest in following any serious topic, to quote my evaluation, "I entered quite readily into some of her diversions, space flight, rodeos, aurora borealis, and the like."

On a later occasion, Mrs. Jones started off by inquiring about my family. I reported their enthusiasm for the rodeo, and this was a subject of interest for her which we pursued for a time. Eventually a lull in the conversation came. Snatches of the verbatim follow:

C-1   "You said earlier that there was nothing about yourself that you'd like to talk about?"

P-1   "I did see Dr. ———— this morning. He said he thought I might be ready to go home about May 1st." (sheepish grin)

C-2   "Does that seem like quite a while? How do you feel about it?"

P-2   "Well, I don't mind. I think he's a good doctor, and I respect his judgment."

C-3   "You are ready to go along with whatever he says."

P-3   "He says I'm better. He said as long as you are here, to keep seeing you."

C-4   "Did he ask you how you felt about that?"

P-4   "No, he just said to keep seeing you."

C-5   "He assumed that it was good for you."

(Silence)

P-9   "I think I may go home to ———— and help my sister-in-law with the children."

P-14   "I think I can be of help to my sister-in-law. They need somebody, and it's something I can do. It will help them a bit financially too if I stay with them."

C-15   "What do you think of that?"

P-15   "I feel it's my duty. He's my brother, and I should help them if I can." (a sheepish grin.)

C-16   "You feel it's your duty? Why did you smile when you said that?"

C-18   "I'll tell you what came to my mind. I didn't think anything about it when you said you felt it was your duty, but when you smiled as you did I began to wonder why and this thought came to me. Is this the same attitude as you had about giving to your mother?"

P-18   "Well, I guess it is, only I feel different about it this time. It's something I can do for them, and it will help me too."

C-19   "It does something for them, but it meets some of your needs too."

Evaluation: (In part)

This verbatim reports some progress, I think, from the standpoint of the patient. She seems to be in good spirits, more confident about the future, more realistic about it, and to be free of any pressing need to talk with me even though an event of some significance had occurred that morning.

This last was apparent when the question of our meeting together for a short time was raised. She said there was nothing she needed to talk about. The value of accepting this statement, yet providing the opportunity by being ready to accept smalltalk, is also illustrated. We had a pleasant time sharing experiences of rodeos. When I drew attention to her earlier statement, she responded by sharing the recent interview with the doctor.

My response at C-2 was not so much to her verbal communication, but to the grin which accompanied it. It was not a good response in that I'm still not sure what she was grinning about. I don't recall any feeling of anxiety at the time of C-4, but I assume that this must have been back of both C-4 and C-5. I didn't sense that she felt these as a bit threatening, but this may well be the reason why she could not continue on this theme.

I was concerned to see what basis in reality there might be for her plan. I was also concerned to know her feelings in the light of the resentment she felt because she had once been expected to provide financial support for her mother. I felt it desirable to make her conscious of her smile which seemed a bit uncalled for. I was a bit hasty in offering a possible interpretation. She didn't acknowledge the correctness of the interpretation, but did respond to the idea that she felt a sense of duty in both situations, but with a difference. She spelled this out as a mutually helpful relationship. I think this is promising. It would seem that her attention was shifting from the hospital toward a purposeful existence beyond.

Some nine days later, in a short session due to another appointment of the patient's, Mrs. Jones typically picked up the conversation with questions focused on me. I shared briefly and moved the conversation back to our common experience of the ward. There were new student nurses about. The patient indicated she had no desire to relive her youth, a sentiment I identified with. Her distress recalled was centered on sex and her mother's ideas about it. She went on to say that she felt she was making progress, however. She reported a recent conversation with Dr. ———— in which he said he thought she was better now than she had been for several years. The occasion for this conversation had been an urgent letter from her sister-in-law requesting help. Mrs. Jones had wanted to go home, but the doctor would only release her for a seven-day visit, so she had decided to send money which would meet the current crisis. My note re her appearance: "the patient looks well, was neatly dressed, hair done up more attractively than formerly. She seemed more confident and light-hearted than most times I have seen her."

The specifics of the next visit were not set down in any detail. Much of it was a topical exchange of information about our educational experiences, through her initiative and with her vocational quest in the background. One paragraph of the summary reads:

"Perhaps the most significant part of the visit had to do with the patient's comparison of her hospitalization in ———— and ————. She had read of the prominent position of the ———— and of what they have been able to do. At the same time, she is happier about her treatment in ————. She characterized the treatment at ———— as 'forced' and that at ———— as 'at your own speed.' She didn't deny the effectiveness of the ———— program, but said it wasn't for her. For the most part I was a listener, but I did ask the occasional question, some of an interpretive nature by implication such as: 'Do you suppose your different experience at ———— and at ———— could have any relation to the degree of your illness at the time?' It was at this point that she said 'no,' the ———— pace was not for her."

Evaluation:

I don't feel that anything of very great moment occurred in this session. It was chiefly interesting for me in that it indicates how patients who are ill are sensitive to and sometimes react against the efforts of others to help them. Undoubtedly some can be speeded toward recovery by aggressive types of therapy, but others will not be hurried and their recovery is only delayed by such efforts. Apparently this patient is one of the latter. My experience with her would tend to confirm that judgment.

Mrs. Jones' growing confidence had been matched by my own progress following psychotherapy. My grasp on this new life of mine was soon to be sorely tested not in relation to my work with Mrs. Jones but in relation to my professional goals. I aspired to be an educator in the field of CPE. No one in all of Western Canada had such qualifications. I saw a vacuum which I thought I could fill. Each March an examining board of the Council of Southwestern Theological Schools interviewed candidates for supervisory training. (The function is now fulfilled exclusively by the Association for Clinical Pastoral Education.) I had applied. A trial run before a group of Houston supervisors had not gone particularly well. When the time came for the all-important meeting, I was conscious of some anxiety but had little awareness of the extent of it. The examining board soon sensed my vulnerability and several members said that I wasn't ready for advanced training. They invited response which came out weak and unconvincing. When more neutral kinds of questions followed, I was still ineffective. The verdict stood. I was judged and found to be not ready.

The hours and the days which immediately followed were exceedingly painful. I was devastated. Even today I can identify with persons who, having experienced rejection for whatever reasons, feel that they are of no account, worthless. The verdict seemed to invalidate my hopes for the future but also seemed to call in question my past and my present usefulness. There were tears and there was sobbing, at times uncontrollable when alone with my wife, and once with my supervisor. How could I go on? My wife, though distressed by my distress and, no doubt, threatened, did not seem to devalue me. My supervisor was understanding and supportive. He did not seem to think that what I had done or what I could do was of no account. My peers treated me much as they always had. Gradually the pain receded, though the problem of my future loomed. With a family to maintain one has to anticipate needs and take action to meet them. A short time later the Institute of Religion offered me the opportunity of staying for a second year, parttime to pursue academic requirements of my over-all program, and parttime in the Counseling Service. Moreover, my hospital community, including my special patient, Mrs.

Jones, continued to receive me as they had always done. My failure to be accepted as a candidate and my humiliation in not functioning well before an examining board I knew did not change my worth in the sight of God. I was back in business again.

My ordeal combined with an extended weekend pass for the patient resulted in the longest break between meetings since I had begun my relationship with Mrs. Jones. Two weeks had intervened without meeting, and it was now six weeks since I had been confronted and had resolved not to lay any expectations or demands on her. I noted that "her appearance was not as good as formerly, her complexion seeming to have erupted in pimples, but she seemed to be in good spirits and was active in the conversation."

The patient was anxious to find out how I had made out before the committee, and I reported on this and on the possibilities for the future. I then inquired about her and her visit to ————. She reported that she had got along well and would like to be discharged soon, for she felt she was needed and that she could make a go of it. However, she seemed to have some uncertainty as to whether the doctor would be prepared to let her go. This proved not to be based on any inquiry or request that she had made, but her own uncertainty about it.

She switched the subject over to the possibilities for me as a marriage counselor and expressed some of her views about the importance of this kind of work. I participated in this.

After a short period of silence she indicated there was something she wanted to share with me but couldn't think of it. I suggested there was no hurry, that she could take the time to think about it if she wanted to. In the meantime she reported something of her sister-in-law's situation, now separated from her husband, the patient's brother.

P-1   "Oh, I know. I must be getting better. Dr. ————
        said about a year ago that as I got better I would begin
        to notice differences in people, that I would find

myself liking some and disliking others, instead of seeing them all alike. Well, (with a grin) I'm beginning to notice that I don't like some people. They bother me. I don't like two or three of the patients who are loud and aggressive. I liked —————, but there are some others who talk too much and too loud."

C-1   "You are beginning to see that people aren't all the same and that's something new for you."

P-2   "Yes, I never used to do that."

C-2   "I wonder how it makes you feel to notice that you like some and dislike others."

P-3   "Oh, pretty good. Another doctor told me one time that you don't like everybody. I know now what he meant."

C-3   "One doctor said that as you got better you would begin to notice differences, likes and dislikes, and another doctor said you can't like everybody. I wonder what they were trying to tell you."

P-4   "Oh, I think they meant that it isn't normal, it isn't healthy not to notice differences, and if you do you can't help but like some and dislike others."

C-4   "This makes sense to you."

P-5   "I think so. I never used to recognize people as individuals. They were just people, especially men."

C-5   "It was as if everybody was pretty much alike, especially men."

P-6   "That's right."

C-6   "Well, I must say I'm surprised. I didn't know that that might be the case. You have made me aware of something I had never realized before. How long do you suppose it has been that you have had difficulty in distinguishing differences?"

P-7   "From my teens, I think."

C-7   "From your teens?"

P-8   "Yes."

C-8   "You mean you have really been unaware of differences all that time?"

P-9   "I don't think I was ever aware of differences the way I am now."

C-9   "You say you have tended to see everybody as pretty much alike, especially men. I wonder how it happens, since you tend to see all men as alike, that we have hit it off as well as we have."

P-10   "I think I have put you on a pedestal."

C-10   "A pedestal? (she nodded) Well, I wonder what it takes to put a man on a pedestal so far as you are concerned."

P-11   (With a little embarrassment) "Proper conduct."

C-11   "I'm not sure that I know what you mean."

P-12   (More embarrassed) ". . . just proper conduct."

C-12   "Perhaps you mean that because I have been satisfied just to talk with you, you have experienced me as different."

P-13   "It wouldn't be so bad if you had an affair with somebody else, just so long as it wasn't me." (blushing)

C-13   "You seem to be rather embarrassed."

P-14   "I guess it's because of the fact that I have fallen so often. I wouldn't want it to happen again."

C-14   "In other words, men are alright so long as they keep their distance."

P-15   "That's about it, I guess."

C-15   "I'm wondering, because you recognize that I am not as you thought all men to be, just how you see men now."

P-16   "I see them differently than I used to. They are not all the same. Now Mr ———, I've told you about him . . . he's different. I think he's interested in me, not sex."

C-16   "I'm not sure I understand."

P-17   "Well, I don't think he's just interested in sex."

C-17   "You mean he's interested in you and not just in using you."

P-18   "Yes."

C-18   "Well, I get the feeling that this is quite a step forward that you have made when you can see people as individuals, and I think I'm about as excited about it as you are. I guess we'll have to call time about now, though."

Evaluation: (In part)

"It would appear that the patient had made a real advance in recent weeks. Some things which she had been told long ago are beginning to be part of her experience. If, as she suggests, she has never before been able to see people really as individuals, this should mean a good deal for her future well-being.

"She sees that I am not like the picture of men which she had had for years, and she is now able to affirm that there are other men who do not fit her previous stereotype. I think this is a good illustration of how therapy or counseling is supposed to work."

Now I see my part largely in terms of reflecting my understanding of her communication and my questioning of her experience without any sense of there being a right answer. As one human being to another, meeting on the basis of equal validity to her experience and to mine, we interacted with one another. Even when she revealed that she put me on a pedestal, I accepted that as her choice with no suggestion that it should be otherwise.

Another summary report preserves the flavor of the interaction and the progress of the patient:

Setting: My first contact with the patient this afternoon was a wave of greeting and an invitation to join the group of which I was a

115

part. She didn't respond to the invitation. There were four patients in the group with me, two quite vocal. However, later when I was seated in the same place with two patients who were more passive and better known to the patient, she joined the group and joined in the conversation. There was a tendency because of the nature of the group for me to be involved in a dialogue with one or another, but there was some genuine group participation in which the patient took part.

I was struck by the patient's appearance, the most noticeable feature being a flushed appearance. She had been to the park the afternoon before and was sunburned. She was with a gentleman friend, by the way. I also felt that her eyes had more of a sparkle, her smile more vivacious, and for the first time I can recall she was wearing lipstick.

When the time came to leave the group and go home, I invited the patient to walk with me and I shared with her my observations. She said that the doctor had noticed her wearing lipstick recently and had remarked that she was doing better. She expressed appreciation of my reporting because she said she was often among the last to recognize changes in herself. She felt that every outing she had boosted her spirits because it increased her confidence about meeting the outside world.

The final record of our relationship during Mrs. Jones' hospital stay now appears as an anticlimax. After some very gentle teasing on my part, we talked about a male friend of the patient, hospitalized for ten years, who was still living in the hospital but holding an important job nearby. Coincidence or not, Mrs. Jones was reminded of a recent dream which she was keen to tell me. There was a girl with a group of prostitutes. She was not one of them, but they seemed to accept her. They were concerned that she should marry and actually helped her to do so. Later the girl was able to provide for the prostitutes so that they no longer had to practice their trade.

Try as I might, I could get her to venture no interpretation or association. She thought that to help prostitutes was a desirable thing to do, and that she would like to do so. She also said that the thought of marriage was not now contrary to her view of herself. She would not however identify herself in the dream, and I, in response to a question about the Bible and dreams, encouraged her to take such meaning from the dream as she could.

Her buoyancy was apparent through recent weeks. She was venturing in relationships and actively anticipating her new life. In relation to me, she conversed much as she had always done. There was, perhaps, a greater freedom on both sides. There may have been a little more initiative from her. That was present in considerable degree throughout, but with more consistency toward the end. For my part, I was consciously trying to be less mechanical, less controlled, more spontaneous. I can't recall having done any teasing such as referred to in this final encounter.

In other respects, though, the dialogue was not reconstructed. The tone of this session seemed very similar to many of its predecessors. I was ready to respond to her agendas in which the focus was on me. I was also alert to the many possibilities for turning the focus to her and her experience. My intent often was to catch the emotional response of the patient to the diverse events and memories which she shared. I was none too accurate, often clumsy in my efforts to draw out the dimensions of her experience, aggressive with my questioning but also ready to accept whatever limited response she put forth. In support of this genuine acceptance, which respected her pace, her control, I noted in my final evaluation this critical reflection. "I felt the proper thing to do was to reflect this interest and draw out associations. Perhaps I was too direct in doing so, for I met with denial of any associations. Then when I eased up the patient did bring forth a concern which I think was an association even if she did not recognize it as such." I had exerted enough pressure that she had to withdraw from it, but when I withdrew the pressure through accepting her denial she volunteered some of her own wonderings, the very process I was committed to fostering.

Mrs. Jones and I had been associating for some seven months. Each of us in our personal worlds had gone through many stressful experiences combining discouragement, anxiety, frustration, and despair. In varying degrees we had shared this with each other. We were both moving into a future with uncertainty and hope. Neither had arrived at the sought-for goal but both had experienced something of a new life which was both a fulfillment and a promise of the life to come. We were on our way!

VI

Did the Gospel Help or Hinder?

In our modern world we are the beneficiaries of a persistent quest for the answers to two basic questions: What happened, and how did it come about? Empirical observation and reflection leads to theorizing, which then is subjected to experimental verification. The religious perspective has tended to be less exact in its perceptions of what has happened and has tended toward a mystical stance in which the activity of God is deemed to be the sufficient answer. As such it is beyond human investigation and control. It cannot be reproduced at will. Failure to produce the desired results experimentally may be seen as confirmation that God was responsible and that only he can repeat it. CPE has recognized the problems associated with living in two different worlds. It has sought to bridge the gap between the scientific and the religious world-view. One expression of this effort in the program in which I was enrolled was the expectation that out of one's clinical work and one's theological framework some thesis might emerge. That is why I undertook consistently to maintain a detailed account of my relationship with Mrs. Jones.

The relationship was now happily ended so far as I could know. She had been discharged with a fair degree of confidence on her part that she was now ready to face life in the world. I had the satisfaction of knowing that I had been intimately involved in her successful hospitalization, feeling, indeed, that I had made a key contribution to her progress.

The doctor confirmed this, but neither of us knew exactly what it was that I had contributed. What thesis could I advance to account for the "what," the greater success in treatment? At the time I had few clues. It took months to come into focus. I knew that I was intrigued by the three obvious phases in the patient's move toward health. That meant there were two periods of transition. What was there in the continuum of her hospitalization which could account for the clinical observation? Could it be some change in relation to the chaplain? Does any Christian understanding or insight seem to be operative?

This is how I assessed the situation. These facts could be substantiated:

(1) The patient, a schizophrenic, paranoid type, was considered to have a poor prognosis.

(2) She had been hospitalized for more than four years, had had several therapists, and a wide range of therapies had been attempted.

(3) She seemed to be resistive to any treatment. Until well into the period of this hospitalization she showed no signs of utilizing the drug thorazine.

(4) Her pattern of recovery included a period of relapse.

Given the facts, there were certain conclusions which seemed to be plausible:

(1) Some new factor must have entered her life which made it possible for the patient to utilize the drug therapy.

(2) That new factor was the chaplain.

(3) The relationship was based, initially, upon the acceptance offered by him as she confessed her sin, acceptance meaning among other things that he took her feelings about sin seriously.

(4) In the absence of any medical reason for the relapse, it was appropriate to look for a clue in the actions or attitude of the chaplain.

(5) It would seem that the chaplain's attitude underwent subtle but significant changes: (a) No confession of the

patient threatened his acceptance of her. He could accept her in spite of her past. (b) He accepted her for what she might become, with implied expectation or demand. (c) He accepted her for what she was, in spite of a future which might not be any different.

Acceptance with implied expectation is not really acceptance. How did all this relate to my theological heritage? Finally, I reached the point where I thought I knew. This was the way I expressed it:

> It is the hypothesis of this study that the doctrine of justification by faith, which, in Protestant thought, is an attempt to formulate the nature of the relationship between God and man which leads to salvation, has important implications for the relationship between pastor and parishioner. Unqualified acceptance of the person as he is, rather than as he may become, and experience by that person that this is so, is a decisive factor in that person's movement toward health.[1]

The doctrine of justification by faith is sometimes viewed as a Reformation phenomenon. It was the watchword of the Reformation, of course, and the emphasis on salvation by faith alone has characterized evangelical Christianity ever since. Contemporary Roman Catholic theologians, however, are moving to reclaim it as part of the historic Catholic faith, submerged for a time, the more so in the wake of the Council of Trent, but part of the earlier tradition.

The most immediate source of the doctrine is in the writings of Saint Paul. In the late nineteenth century it was a fashion among scholars to regard it as a distinctly Pauline creation, a distortion of the simple gospel proclaimed by Jesus of Nazareth. This view is no longer widely held. Paul gave it its classic expression, but the truth he proclaimed was implicit in what Jesus did and deeply rooted in the heritage of Israel.

The clearest and most concise scriptural reference to it is found in Romans 1:16-17, "For I am not ashamed of the gospel: it is the power of God for salvation to every one who has faith, to the Jew first and also to the Greek. For in it the righteousness of God is revealed through faith for faith; as it is written, 'He who through faith is righteous shall live.' "

Our English translations inevitably conceal the relationship between righteousness and justification. The older King James version at least made the connection more apparent with its "The just shall live by faith." The fact is that the words which may be translated as "just" or "justify," from whence the concept of justification is derived, may as correctly be translated as "righteous" and "righteousness." I have N. H. Snaith, veteran biblical scholar, as authority for the statement that apart from three references, all in the book of Proverbs, this is true for the whole of the Old Testament as well as the New.[2] To be justified means to be brought into a right relationship with a person. It can apply to relationships between human beings. It can refer to the relationship between the human and the divine. In the former instance the basis for it is in the actions of the two parties. In the latter the dependence is all upon God. The doctrine of justification by faith is a declaration, then, of what God has done to bring the human race into a right relationship with himself.

What Paul had in mind was a specific event in time, the life, death, and resurrection of Jesus. We can't really appreciate what he understood by justification, or righteousness, however, without some further reference to history. Central to all Hebrew thinking about God was the concept of justice. He is the one who is the author of justice, who acts justly. He it is who gives the Law, who rewards goodness and punishes wrongdoing. He is the model by which mortals are to conduct their ways with one another. Hence the prophets with their denunciations of violence, exploitation, and neglect were pointing to the norms of God's dealings with his people, and insisting that because those norms were of the very nature of God, he must surely act in the face of injustice for all, including the widow and the fatherless. God is the vindicator. He is the savior of his people, both the norm and the agent of justice.

Because he was the norm, or the model, of justice and ethical action, and because his people were called to be like him in that respect, it was very easy to assume that anyone fulfilling such ethical requirements was righteous, that their relationship with God was secured because of their performance of good works. A popular Christian view of Old Testament religion, not an accurate one, is that it was a religion of works, that individuals earn their own salvation. There is, of course, some basis for such an appraisal. Popular religion always evolves. It strays beyond the bounds of its source, adding new dimensions and distorting old beliefs. With the passing of the centuries, the vissitudes of history, the prominence of oral tradition and rabbinic interpretations of it, it is understandable that greater emphasis would come to rest on human response and a system of rewards and punishments be made the basis of God's relationship with his creatures. Hence a person would be perceived as in a right relationship with him if that person observed the Law in all its fullness. The righteousness of the expected messiah was conceived in terms of perfect obedience to the Law of God (one reason why Jesus didn't seem to fit). Everyone must strive in order to be judged righteous. Woe unto those who in the Last Judgment are not so found. Though prophetic religion called out for ethical behavior and was the upholder of moral values, by contrast, it affirmed, along with the judgment of God, the mercy of God and utter dependence upon him in any relationship with him. Justification, in other words, is due not to any human initiative or action but solely to the character and power of God. That is the background for Paul's proclamation so concisely stated, "He who through faith is righteous shall live." The major statement of his case is in the letter to the Romans, especially the first four chapters. There are other significant supporting references in Corinthians, Philippians, and, notably, Galatians, chapters two and three.

"In it [the gospel] the righteousness of God is revealed through faith for faith" (Rom. 1:17). What is the appropriate understanding of the righteousness of God in this context? It could be understood as the righteousness that God would have from his people. As such it would be a response to the persistent human question, "How can I become righteous before God?" The answer would therefore be, "Have faith." For large numbers of people whom I have known that is no more good news than is the demand to keep the Law. Meeting the requirement is beyond them. Is there, then, no hope of justification?

Fortunately, there is another understanding of the phrase. It may not refer to any ethical or religious achievement of the individual, but rather to the righteousness of God himself. Here is what Martin Luther, preeminent among interpreters of Paul, has to say:

> Only the gospel reveals the righteousness of God, i.e. who is righteous before God by that faith alone by which one believes the word of God . . . for the righteousness of God is the cause of salvation. Here, too, the righteousness of God must not be understood as the righteousness by which He is righteous in Himself, but as the righteousness by which we are made righteous (justified) by Him, and this happens through faith in the gospel.[3]

Luther continued by contrasting the view of Aristotle, that righteousness followed upon and flowed from action, with the understanding of Christian revelation, that "righteousness precedes works and works proceed from it." "Similarly," he declared, "no one can perform the works of a bishop or priest unless he is first consecrated and sanctified to such an office; righteous works of men who are not yet righteous can thus be likened to the works of someone who performs the functions of a priest or bishop although he is far from being a priest; in other words, such works are foolish and done for sport, and resemble the doings of circus entertainers."[4]

There can be no doubt about Luther's stand. The righteousness of God refers to no goal, virtue, or achievement from the human side of the divine-human relationship. The reference is to God. Contemporary interpreters, among them J. A. Bollier, agree.[5]

It would be wrong to think of this righteousness of God

solely as an attribute, a quality, or characteristic of the divine being. That doesn't have the dynamic which was part of the biblical view. In today's language, it may be helpful to think of it as referring to an action, a process. The basic concept of Hebrew religion was covenant. The righteousness of God was in the relationship of his people. "He is just who does justice to the claims made upon him in the name of a relationship. Thus God's righteousness is manifested first in that he rules according to the covenant in fellowship with his people."[6] So God's righteousness consists of doing what he agreed to do, establishing justice, preserving the nation from enemies within and without. It is inherent not in his person alone, but in relationship, or, as John Knox puts it: "It designates not so much God's righteousness as an act of God on behalf of men."[7]

The good news for which Paul makes no apology is that God has acted in response to the need of his covenant people. He has acted through the life, death, and resurrection of Jesus of Nazareth. To know that, to accept it as true, to believe, to have faith in him is to know that we are righteous (justified) and to experience a power for good works which is none other than the power of God. It is to receive new life, making the language of death and resurrection descriptive of the experience of those who receive it. "This is the Lord's doing; it is marvelous in our eyes" (Ps. 118:23; Mark 12:11).

This is the "what" of modern empirical inquiry. Can we say anything about the "how"? I think we can, at least tentatively, identify some such understanding in the thought of Paul. The first evidence of God's saving grace which he cites is his judgment. "For the wrath of God is revealed from heaven against all ungodliness and wickedness of men" (Rom. 1:18). The argument that unfolds in chapters two and three is to the effect that the whole human race, both Jews and Gentiles, has fallen under the judgment of God and all are helpless and hopeless to save themselves. Paul's own heroic and desperate bid as a Pharisee to keep the Law is part of the background as is his failure to gain peace. So also are the evidences of evil on every hand, the pain and the suffering, the trouble and sorrow, the sin and shame. In Paul's thinking, the lamentable state of human affairs was both occasion for the wrath of God and the expression of it.

For Paul, of course, the wrath of God did not represent a capricious, irrational, erratic rage but a consistent, active, and purposeful opposition to evil. It was the dark side of his righteousness. The very circumstances which Paul deplored were also the occasion for believing that God was alive and at work to bring justice and righteousness and peace to his world. Karl Barth in his exposition of Romans 1:17 states that because God is who he is, namely, righteous, he had to act.[8] He had made men for fellowship with himself, and when that fellowship was broken he had to act to restore it. To give man free rein, to let evil abound, to let the gulf between man and himself grow wider and wider, to wink indefinitely at evil, would not be to be God. Therefore to be himself, he must bring his people under judgment. In so doing, he shows that he is committed to the covenant and is actively at work to overcome the gulf between himself and his creatures which has resulted from their sin. God is faithful, loyal, true, in contrast to the waywardness of both Jews and Gentiles. The nature of the judgment made against them is thus highlighted: Their unrighteousness consists in their lack of faithfulness, in their turning aside from God, in their failure to seek after him (cf. Rom. 1:18-23).

Jesus is at once the model of righteousness, of fellowship with God and trust in him. By what he taught and by the way he lived, he exposed the failures of his contemporaries and in his death witnessed to his own faithfulness and to the seriousness with which God views human sin. God's action in Jesus is then, first, an act of judgment, without which he could not be the covenant God.

A second feature of God's action on our behalf is identifiable in these words: "But now the righteousness of God has been manifested apart from the law, although the law and the prophets bear witness to it, the righteousness of God through faith in Jesus Christ for all who believe" (Rom. 3:21-22). This is not judgment. It is not the abrogation of judgment. It presupposes the reality of it as part of God's action, but another dimension seems indicated. It either follows judgment or is concurrent with it. Of what does it consist?

The righteousness of God is used in yet another sense. John Knox tries to catch the meaning of this usage in these words: "The state of approvedness, the character of being declared righteous, of being acquitted, which God alone can confer."[9] It is like a status conferred in response to faith, to all who believe.

Paul tried to explain further:

For there is no distinction; since all have sinned and fall short of the glory of God, they are justified by his grace as a gift, through the redemption which is in Christ Jesus, whom God put forth as an expiation by his blood, to be received by faith. This was to show God's righteousness, because in his divine forbearance he had passed over former sins; it was to prove at this present time that he himself is righteous and that he justifies him who has faith in Jesus. (Rom. 3:22-26)

In other words, along with the judgment God offers a gift. Man is not righteous, nor for all his striving can he become so. He can be justified (i.e., made righteous) only by the gracious act of God in the person of Jesus Christ, in his life and death and resurrection. Justification is a gift, an unconditional gift, equally available to everyone, there for the taking. God declares us to be righteous. His action is appropriated by faith. "He who through faith is righteous shall live" (Rom. 1:17).

It is not an easy matter to accept this. We are very much like the ancient Jews who were convinced that their part in the covenant was to keep the divine law. They knew by experience that as a nation, and even as individuals, they never could achieve that. Some, rather than despair, concluded that it might suffice to know the law, others that to be a descendant of Abraham, symbolized by circumcision, was a sufficient guarantee of the desired relationship with God. We tend to think and feel as if we were operating under the same dispensation. Even when we make profession of faith, we sometimes act as if we are not righteous. We confuse being "righteous" with being "virtuous." If we experience ourselves as having sinned and as still being in the clutches of self-centeredness and ineffectiveness, how then can we be righteous? Even if we are treated as righteous, are we not yet guilty?

The persistence of this nagging thought may be traced, in the view of some scholars, to the fact that many theologians of the past, including the Reformers, believed that we live under a universal law which requires satisfaction for sin. In this view Christ's death provided the satisfaction, so persons could be accounted righteous, with faith taking the place of actual righteousness. Modern interpreters, Karl Barth, C. K. Barrett, and Anders Nygren among them, understand Paul to say that faith is righteousness before God, justification an act of forgiveness on God's part, a creative act by which the believer is made righteous, a participant in the righteousness of God.

That is the gift of God which comes to us through faith in Jesus Christ. There is still a problem here. Some people have faith and some don't. Some people who profess to having faith don't experience the new life of freedom and power which in the New Testament is associated with faith in Jesus Christ. In fact, today, many Protestants are engaged in the same frantic struggle to do what is required of them, despite their knowledge of justification by faith, and many Catholics the same. Faith can't be, therefore, a profession of faith nor any other calculated effort on the part of the believer. Otherwise it partakes of the same order as other attempts to become righteous. It is self-defeating.

The faith which saves is itself part of the gift. It is God's doing. It comes when and if God is ready to give it. That does not remove the problem entirely, nor was Paul unaware of the difficulty with that kind of answer. He was painfully aware that most of his fellow-Jews had not responded to the preaching of the gospel. In Romans, chapters nine through eleven, he discusses the possibility that God has cast away his people. He concludes that this is not the case, that God in his own time will bring them: "a hardening has come upon part of Israel, until the full number of the Gentiles come in, and so all Israel will be saved" (Rom. 11:25-26). Not even the ability to respond is our achievement. That, too, is God's doing. When it happens we give God the praise.

The whole spirit of the Letter to the Romans, the key to its interpretation, is to be found in the contrast between theocentric and egocentric fellowship with God. Making this point Anders Nygren quotes Luther as follows:

"Here it is vital that our own righteousness and wisdom be brought to naught and rooted out of our hearts," and again "God will not save us through our own righteousness and wisdom but through a righteousness which has neither come from us or been produced by us, but which has come to us from elsewhere, which did not grow on earth but comes from heaven."[10]

The Reality of Judgment

When Paul prepared to go to Rome he wrote the Letter to the Romans as his personal introduction. He sent forth a comprehensive statement of his understanding of the gospel. It began with man's universal need, the need for reconciliation with God, which had arisen through man's refusal and failure to live according to God's purpose. For him the distress so apparent in the world was the consequence of human disobedience and, at the same time, evidence of God's activity to restore a right relationship with himself. Judgment, the wrath of God, in his view was the starting point of the good news.

It is not difficult to see in the life of Mrs. Jones a specific example of Paul's diagnosis of the universal human need. Outward circumstances and her own reaction to those circumstances fashioned a web which slowly but surely deprived her of her freedom and all but destroyed her as a person. It is not possible to draw precise lines of responsibility between her parents, her family, the community, and herself. Nevertheless, collectively, they were responsible for untold trouble and sorrow of which the sufferings of the patient were only a small part. The details of their human experience make sordid and distressful reading, just like the biblical description of the plight of the human race which has turned away from God.

Judgment is a thread which runs through the narrative of Mrs. Jones's life. Her family was at the bottom of the social scale in its small home community. She experienced the low esteem in which her family was held. She knew that her brothers did not meet community norms. She herself was incriminated through the sexual initiatives of a brother, punished, and humiliated, especially in her own eyes. On two occasions she had experienced God and knew some peace and sense of well-being, but the relief was of short duration. She felt judged and rejected by others, increasingly isolated from all fellow human beings, and guilty before God. In addition to matters of social background and morality, she came to experience judgment in reference to personal achievement, perceptions of reality, health. Whatever the criteria, she ended up feeling that she was sadly deficient and condemned to oblivion.

Her experience of judgment was reported to me first and foremost as the judgment of God. Her reporting of it revealed some ambivalence. She knew the content of Christian teaching regarding forgiveness and that, in her better moments, took some of the sharpness and the terror of his judgment away. Her experience of it and her dread of future judgment committed her to anxiety and fear and rendered her incapable of any sustained and rational evaluation of her experience of judgment or of her perception of God and of his will. She tended to accept uncritically her inherited childhood concepts, whatever their source.

Her church involvement had been slight, varied, and usually brief. She accepted that churches have standards which should be maintained. Yet she was attracted to the

Catholic church because it seemed to be more accepting of sinners. She was distressed by the practice of some churches who "read" people out of the church because of alleged moral lapses. Her church demanded that she confess in order to be reinstated and thereby made eligible for her letter of transfer. She was more impressed by the standards than she was by the acceptance offered by the churches.

Though she did find a haven in the hospital, she did not escape the experience of judgment there either. They didn't condemn her for her past. Their expectations of her seemed not to be the same as in the churches. The standards seemed different. They didn't talk of God and, it would seem, there was no way that she could relate their standards to the standards of the God whose judgment she feared. She didn't see how they could ignore sin. As she put it, "They don't believe in sin." She had not read Hobart Mowrer's *The Crisis in Psychiatry and Religion,* in which he maintained that patients who feel guilty are, in fact, guilty.[11] Nor could she have known that Dr. Karl Menninger, renowned psychiatrist, would write a book called *Whatever Became of Sin?*[12] I have no way of knowing what her several doctors thought about this subject. In fairness to them I must allow that her perceptions of their attitudes could have been distorted. All that can be said is that the patient's perceptions of their attitudes were to the effect that "it doesn't matter," "do whatever you feel like doing," "don't feel guilty for what you choose to do." Her reporting suggests that they failed to accept her as a person who could not see herself apart from her guilt.

In the hospital she continued to experience judgment, to feel unacceptable because of her guilt feelings, her religious beliefs, and her lack of productivity in psychotherapy. She confused fantasy and reality and pressed for discharge from time to time.

There was also the experience of judgment in relation to me. She readily received me as a minister, or pastor, representing God. For her, I am sure, there was both promise and threat in such a relationship. There was also the possibility of disappointment, condemnation, admonition, or rejection. Several of the early encounters were occasions for testing. She took positions which might have been the occasion for conflict, for example, baptism, confession, church discipline. While she knew that there was no clear agreement between us in these matters, indeed some evidence of disagreement, she did not experience rejection. The relationship remained in spite of our differences.

The same was true with respect to my attitude toward her guilt. I was respectful and accepting of her with her related religious ideas and conceptions about sin. I'm sure she experienced areas of agreement as well as areas of disagreement in regard to specifics, for example, God's purpose for sex, but with it all she must have experienced a message of genuine acceptance of her which was qualitatively different from the acceptance of her medical therapist at this point. Or was the difference in my representative role, beyond the personal and the professional, in the realm of the divine? In that case it would not be what I said or didn't say but who I was in her eyes which made the difference.

Certainly, I was uneasy expressing some of the views I did and uneasy about answering in a factual way some of the biblical questions which she posed to me. I knew that opinions and texts could be experienced as judgments, that they could be threats to our continuing relationship as judgmental statements can so often be. Even if not so decisive, they may still seal off areas of sensitivity which might otherwise be shared. I tried to duck incriminating questions by turning them back to her to get behind the presenting question to the concern which lay back of it. Yet there was enough of the traditional pastor in me that I did venture information and opinions related to scripture which may have been experienced as judgment. Included among them was my implicit assumption, sometimes more or less overt, that she should be different, able to accept God's forgiveness, able to venture forth with greater faith, able to trust others and love herself. Yet the relationship remained.

The other way in which judgment appeared was in the reevaluation of her life experience which went on throughout most of our time together. In between sessions, as she reported it, she was reliving much of her past, recalling experiences long since forgotten, making connections between her past and her present which therapists had urged upon her on previous occasions but which had then gone unheeded. She was reassessing experiences such as the voice of God telling her not to eat. She was recognizing that much of her past behavior was dictated by the desire to satisfy others, not God. She was finding reasons for appreciating the doctors and what they had tried to do. She was reassessing some of her earlier perceptions of me, able to see that I was somewhat reserved as she was reserved, and able to tell me, be it somewhat covertly, that she would like to be treated differently.

Judgment is not a bad word in Christian faith. Nor is it in therapy. There is, indeed, no escape from it. The word needs to be rescued from its association with condemnation and with judgmental attitudes which convey on the one hand blame, guilt, and shame, and on the other pride, superiority, and power.

The Reality of Forgiveness

What prevents judgment from being bad news? In the context of Paul's exposition of the Christian faith in Romans, that which makes judgment part of the good news is that it is coupled with an unconditional caring, which is not vindictive, which is not passive patience and suffering while the human race smartens up, but is, instead, an active and powerful force restoring broken relationships between person and person, nation and nation. What no one by dint of effort has been able to do is now possible through God's action in Jesus Christ. The individual who appropriates the fruits of this action finds new life with power, through faith, itself God's gift.

The futility of Mrs. Jones's effort to rescue herself from experienced alienation and rejection is apparent. Born to an impoverished family, deprived of the very real advantages of a stable home life, early handicapped by lack of respect from the wider community and by her own guilt and shame, she had tried to win recognition. She had excelled in sports. She prided herself in her morals. She was born again, according to the standards of revivalist religion. She slipped from grace. She was reborn in keeping with the standards of the local church. She ventured into personal relationships. She married. She sought a career. She sought the help of doctors. Nothing satisfied her deeper needs. No one could help her in her guilt and hopelessness. Even her professed religious beliefs were of no avail.

Somehow she had missed the unconditional caring which in spite of the judgment offers a relationship of love and trust. God, through Jesus Christ, had granted forgiveness but she had not received it. She could accept as history God's action in Christ on her behalf, but she could not appropriate God's continuing activity on her behalf.

In traditional terms, she had experienced the wrath of God but nothing comparable to the unconditional caring which the early Christians knew through the life and death and resurrection of Jesus. She associated the church with caring but also with moral standards which they upheld by reading people out of their membership. Her experience of them had always been of fear. She associated the hospital with caring but in her experience the doctors didn't understand guilt and when, in their opinion, she could not benefit from further psychotherapy, they consigned her to a regime of medication. She had not been able to use what they had offered. Her personal relationships tended to be brief, whether through her own actions or through the givenness of the medical and institutional establishment.

In the chaplain she found acceptance in spite of the sorry

past which she related bit by bit. In him she found acceptance in spite of the guilt to which she seemed to cling so tenaciously. He accepted her though he could not understand how she could proclaim her faith in God and his righteousness, in his mercy and love, and exclude herself from among the beneficiaries. Differences in doctrine, differences in scriptural interpretation, differences in understanding of Christan moral imperatives seem not to have intervened to seriously threaten continuing fellowship. The differences were there, overt and covert, but she continued to feel good about what was happening between them even when outward signs suggested that she was having trouble. He didn't seem upset by the apparent reversal of her progress. The chaplain assumed many initiatives and was elusive, if not manipulative, at times. His maneuvers, however, had a permissive and sometimes playful quality about them which made it easy for her to turn aside from anything she did not want to deal with and still feel she would be accepted.

Yet there was one respect in which she did feel uncomfortable. She did experience less than full acceptance. She felt some expectation and implied demand that she should get better, improve, change, be different. Even though she protested, she felt sure that the intentions were good. She experienced my expectations as caring. Judgment and caring were integrated once again, as they must have been on many earlier occasions. Since this particular meeting was a turning point for her, what made it different?

My first impression, which has endured to the time of this writing, was that when challenged to abandon my expectations for change in her, to offer an unconditional caring, I changed my attitude toward her in our times together and with that burden removed she was able to resume her progress once more. She said all along that her sessions with me continued to be helpful. What she reported of her inner life seemed to make that a plausible belief. But something clearly had detracted from her sense of well-being, had submerged the evidence of progress, even though it had not really blocked it. My impression may be true absolutely or it may be, and this is my present conclusion, that my change was a secondary factor.

I think there is good reason to believe that in the midst of relapse when she was reliving so much of her past and continuing to make new discoveries, all of which had relevance for her present and her future, she was even then functioning in the awareness that she lived in a relationship with God, represented through our relationship, combining judgment and acceptance. Out of that growing awareness, I conclude she found the security and the confidence to claim, as she did, her right to be accepted as a person. It was an act of self-affirmation. It was a proclamation of something which had already happened. She had come to accept herself, not as a desperate act, breathing defiance toward a critical and unfriendly world, but as a quiet, gentle, and sincere response to what, in her head, she had known all along, namely, the gospel of Jesus Christ. I couldn't say exactly, nor could she say, I am sure, just when the gospel had actually been received.

The Reality of the Promise

"He who through faith is righteous shall live." The reference is to a new quality of life. When the Bible speaks of life it seldom does so in terms of mere existence. Humanity shares physical existence with all God's creaturely creation, but it is of his human handiwork that it is said he breathed into them the breath of life. Life has a Godward connotation. It is life lived in relationship to God. Sheol, the place of departed spirits, was dreaded by the early Hebrews not because of anticipated punishment (that came later) but because it was life without God, existence without life. It is in that sense that we may understand the promise of life. Whereas those who turn away from God and those who rely on their own efforts to achieve a relationship with him are subjected to all manner of evil and futility, those who accept his gift of righteousness shall receive a new order of existence, a new quality of life. There was no mistaking this in the story of the church. A group of disheartened and leaderless followers of Jesus was transformed into a committed and triumphant band. Dedicated but desperate men like Saul were turned around to become, like Paul, confident and courageous apostles of peace and concord. A handful of powerless people, armed only with the gospel, soon acquired the reputation of having turned the world upside down. That is the connotation of life. That is the promise in the doctrine of justification by faith. It is an immediate possession, an existential experience after which the self and the world seem different. That is not the end of the promise. What is gained immediately through the gift of faith points beyond itself. New life is present and future. Resurrection experienced now is a reality beyond physical death. God's power has been manifested in our life. It will be manifested as the days unfold. We are still in the world and subject to its conditions which are far from the conditions of the kingdom of God, but he is at work and his gracious will shall one day prevail.

In passing, be it noted that health in the Bible is used in a parallel way. Health in our world is so often defined in negative terms, i.e., the absence of disease. In scripture it is assumed that health is a positive quality of life, much to be desired and sought after, but unlike modern medical definitions of it, it was understood to include a right relationship with God. Health and salvation belong together. They bespeak the same quality of life.

The most striking feature of Mrs. Jones's life during the early months of her relationship with me was the change in her physical condition and accompanying social function. Medically she was on the same regime as on previous recent admissions. This time she began to put on weight, a typical response to thorazine, previously absent from her history. Her eating and sleeping patterns improved. She was more frequently a participant in ward activities. She was eager to meet and to pursue her agenda with me. She reported her growing awareness of change, her growing optimism that help was at hand. Much of the talk was God-talk. Implicit in it was faith in a righteous and loving God who forgives. Was the new quality of life the fruit of faith? Was it a gift from God? I believe it was.

Nor was that new quality of life based on faith entirely lost. It was submerged for a time, not so much because of guilt but because of her continuing sense of confusion, lack of direction, and fear. How could God value a rudderless ship drifting helplessly, with no past record of performance, shackled by past failures, and with no prospect of any different future?

I suppose her predicament was that of a new plateau with higher ground yet to be achieved, the initial success exhilarating but the ultimate goal still looming in the distance with very real hazards in between. The natural reaction is to recoil, to shrink back, to cling to whatever security remains from the old and familiar way of life. If the old identity, the old view of the self is given up, what will the new one be? Will it really serve as well? When acceptance is experienced a new form of the self arises and the person begins to question who he or she really is. Is the self ready to face the questions? Can the self really accept the new view? Is it able to cope with the strengths and the weaknesses which may be revealed? It is an awesome prospect for anyone, with possibilities and responsibilities enough to stagger the imagination, even as Mrs. Jones one time remarked.

Seward Hiltner has commented on this stage both in therapy and in pastoral work. Previously, he says, the energy of the person has been directed toward defending something unacceptable in himself. When this is accepted these energies must be used in some way other than concealing or fighting the unacceptable. There opens up a whole range of new possibilities and these new options threaten because they cannot be ignored. What is ultimately liberating may be very threatening in the short term, especially if there is any suggestion of coercion.[13]

Though Mrs Jones's spiral downward was evident and its causes were not apparent, she continued to use the security gained through her relationship with me to reexamine her past and to reflect on her present, until one day she affirmed herself as acceptable, a person of worth despite her limitations. The courage to do so was another response of faith leading to another step into life. It was another gift by which she was able to move forward once more.

The person who finds the courage to accept acceptance, in Paul Tillich's phrase, finds an exciting new life ahead. Daniel Day Williams in his book *The Minister and the Care of Souls* shares case material in which a client toward the end of counseling expresses her feelings in these terms, "rejoice and be exceedingly glad" (Matt. 5:12). It isn't that all the pieces had fallen into place at last. Quite the contrary. What happens, according to the summary of the counselor, is:

(1) That the client discovers that recognizing an experience for what it is constitutes a more effective method of meeting life than does the denial or distortion of experience.

(2) The client discovers that what has been needed is a love that is not possessive, which demands no personal gratification.

(3) There is the discovery that there is at the core of one's being nothing dire or destructive of self, and nothing damaging, or possessing, or warping of others.

(4) The client comes to feel that it is possible to walk with serenity through a world that seemes to be falling to pieces.[14]

Mrs. Jones did not articulate as this client did, but her mood during those last days in hospital was essentially the same. The clouds had not all dissipated. Her handicaps were still real and the future was still filled with unanswered and unanswerable questions. But much had happened to her. She knew that life had been transformed, that it could never be the same again. The victories won gave promise of greater victories. The future might continue to loom, but she could face it without despair and with a joy which previously had been only a part of her religious vocabulary but which she now possessed as a gift.

I conclude that there is a very close parallel between the experience represented by the doctrine of justification by faith and the experience of therapy as represented by my work with Mrs Jones. I was not a traditional therapist and at times eschewed the name. That there was a therapeutic relationship seems to be beyond dispute. I was not a faith-healer as that term is commonly understood. To say that I was a healer of faith, that I helped her to reinterpret her experience of life and to discover what was true all along, would be a more accurate description of my function. I helped to make real for her the reality of a caring relationship which makes no absolute demands even though judgment is implicit in it. I pointed beyond myself and the human context to the God who revealed himself in his unconditional caring through Jesus Christ. I was a minister.

VII

My Ministry and Me

In the context of my development as a professional minister, my relationship with Mrs. Jones has had a salutary effect. It confirmed me as a person whose gifts God could use in ministering to other persons. I knew I had not been very skillful. I knew that I had no understanding or knowledge by which I could take credit for the transformation which was taking place. Yet I felt a part of it. Though I knew myself to be justified by faith and not by works, I celebrated that sense of participation in a significant process. My confidence for the future was bolstered. I was eager to pursue opportunities by which I could further be used by God to help and to heal.

I was also puzzled and curious to understand more of the dynamics which might account for the history of Mrs. Jones's journey toward health and salvation. When through my own choice, in pursuit of my studies, I was confronted by the doctrine of justification by faith and subsequently related it to my work with Mrs. Jones, I felt excited and affirmed. Not only did I produce a thesis which, when accepted, completed the requirements for my Master's degree, but I had the profound satisfaction of knowing that in my counseling and caring ministry I could function with integrity. Being a representative of the Christian faith, I knew that tradition-ally meant being an upholder of values, or of morality, a teacher and advocate, a symbol of God's judgment and of his saving love. My preaching and my practice could be integrated into one function, a wholeness, which is ministry.

Further, I came to feel that I had a perspective to share with my fellow clergy, a ministry to them.

During my second year I experienced further growth through my academic program and my work in a counseling service. My sense of competence as a counselor grew as I saw what could happen in the lives of others who chose to sit down with me in search of solutions to their very human problems. When Edward Thornton used case material from my counseling in his book *Theology and Pastoral Counseling* and described me a seasoned minister of the United Church of Canada, I also experienced a lift.[1] With a growing sense of my own worth and authority as a person, I eventually met the same examining board which a year earlier had examined me and found me wanting. This time I was accepted as a supervisor of CPE in training. After twenty-seven months of graduate training I returned to Canada, excited, expectant, because of the progress made and the possibilities for a new career as an educator.

I was not to be spared the pitfalls, however. I was to find that the lesson which seemed so clear from my work with Mrs. Jones was not established forever in my functioning. When I moved to Vancouver, British Columbia, with a mandate from my denomination to be a hospital chaplain and to work toward establishment of a program of CPE, I found that the hospital situation was not conducive to such a program at that time. Not only was there an administration which was cautious, resistive to change, and uninformed about modern concepts of hospital ministry, there were also three denominational chaplains of greater vintage than myself on the scene, two of them reluctant to change the status quo. The Council of Churches was no better informed than the hospital and was not ready to recognize any other pattern than the one already operative. Though some were impressed by my skills and enthusiasm, I suffered disappointment and setback. There were long months of frustration. I accumulated feelings of resentment directed toward my fellow chaplains. The more I pressed for change the more they resisted. The day came when I recognized the futility of what I was doing. I confessed to God my resentment and scorn, and my inability to regard them as my peers. I made the same kind of confession, in effect, that I had done in the presence of Mrs. Jones. I had failed to treat them as persons of worth, failed to accept them as I experienced them. My needs and expectations had crowded in to limit and obstruct my relationship with them. I was suffering the very real consequences of my sin. When I started again to try to show my acceptance of them as persons, with different histories and different gifts, to be sure, but nonetheless God's creatures, persons of worth in his sight, new developments began to take place. Some attitudes softened. We recognized the differences, the somewhat conflicting interests and needs, but we dealt with each other as one person meeting another rather than as one impersonal and immovable force meeting another immovable force. The way was open to further change though none of us knew exactly where that might take us.

It seems there are some things I cannot repeat to myself too often. One of those is certainly the importance of the doctrine of justification by faith for ministry. In every part of the traditional work of the ministry it sheds light. It addresses itself very much to the problems of ministry as identified by Henri Nouwen, the resistances to learning from the minister as teacher, the resistances to change through the call to repentance from the preacher or through exhortations to good works from the same source. The doctrine of justification by faith offers a diagnosis and a prescription for the minister who can't understand why persons seek counsel yet seem to make so little use of it. Organizational problems are real in the work of the Christian ministry, so much so that administration for many has become a bad word. As for the experience of worship as a duty rather than a celebration, it may be that there would be more to celebrate if there were a more constant awareness of what the doctrine is all about.

I see this doctrine as a shorthand diagnosis of the human

situation. That diagnosis has to do with self-centeredness and estrangement from God. Justification by faith outlines the treatment, the task of ministry, which is to prepare the way so that God may enter with his reconciling and empowering love.

Judgment is a part of that preparation. For a long time pastoral care, using the model of psychology as a developing science, shied away from the idea that a pastor's judgment had any place in the helping process. To appear to be indifferent or permissive in an attempt to avoid making judgments is to avoid genuine encounter and can be destructive. Only through judgments consciously made can the pastor be helpful. The problem arises when the pastor's judgments show through, as inevitably they will, outside of personal awareness. Such mistakes need not be irretrievable if they can be acknowledged and confessed, for this implies that the pastor, too, is under judgment and, like the client, may stand in need of forgiveness.

I like what Samuel Southard writes:

The pastor's awareness of his own judgments does not mean immediate condemnation of his parishioner or himself. The personal convictions of a Christian stand under God's judgment and are continually subject to reappraisal. The counselor who says he can never pass judgment on another individual may never have solved the problem of God's judgment upon his own life. He may fear that his own opinions would get out of control and he would act in the place of a god before others. If this is so, it should be examined. If, on the other hand, the counselor knows from personal experience that he is under God's judgment, then with humility and faith he can present his own conviction in a spirit of love and self-control.[2]

This implies that humility is of considerable importance. It means that when a judgment is shared about another person it should be in the form of a contribution to the judgments already being made by that person and that the judgments of that person must also be recognized as having paramount importance for the growth of the relationship.

Acceptance, as I understand it, is not approval or disapproval of behavior or emotion. It is not assent or dissent to propositions. I know how hard I had to struggle with that realization. I found it hard to put myself into a perspective which freed me from the necessity of giving my opinion or feelings. Acceptance is, as Carl Rogers writes, "the creation of an atmosphere in which the client can come to recognize that he has negative feelings and can accept them as part of himself."[3] It is positive regard in spite of that which might be the occasion for offense. In Seward Hiltner's phrase, "acceptance does not necessarily mean agreement. It means accepting the person through the one thing that makes it possible at the time namely, accepting the very feeling that threatens the relationship."[4]

I find it hard to conceptualize and to make explicit the subtleties implicit in both Rogers' and Hiltner's statements. Understandably the reference is to the thoughts, emotions, and actions of another person. Under normal human conditions what another person says, does, or feels is intimately bound up with his or her sense of selfhood, and rejection at any of these levels may be perceived as rejection of the self. Rejection of negative feelings may block an adequate experience of those dimensions of the self and an adequate reappraisal of previous judgments concerning them.

There is another side to the equation, however, and that is the response of the receiver. This will depend on the self-awareness of the receiver and the sense of separation that can be maintained. Another way of expressing this element might be to point out that no one outside the self can be held responsible for what the self experiences. Much of counseling is devoted to helping the troubled individual discover the nature of personal responsibility and the choices that are available. By the same token, in the face of the thoughts, words, and actions of the other person, the receiver may experience a range of reactions but is not thereby a victim. The receiver may well take note of the feelings induced but then has the further responsibility to use those feelings in the interests of the relationship. It may be that the first response and the only appropriate one is to say to oneself, "What the other has said causes me discomfort. I accept myself with my discomfort. I don't have to act to relieve my discomfort. I can accept the other person because I can accept myself with my discomfort."

On another occasion I might think it appropriate to recognize that I am responsible for whatever discomfort I experience and that it is not the responsibility of the other person to spare me from such emotions. Instead of exercising the option previously mentioned of dealing with the feelings in a purely internal fashion, I might share with the other person my discomfort, taking care not to attach blame, for that would be denying my responsibility for what I feel. In doing so it would be important by word or by manner to make it clear that the relationship means more to me than the discomfort, that I value or accept the other in spite of my negative feelings, and that I make no demand and exercise no power to force a change.

What this points to, I think, is something which is made explicit in relation to family therapy but not in discussions of acceptance which I have heard. The problem is not the fault of one party or the other. The problem is in the relationship and the person who would be accepting of the other must be as open to recognizing and accepting whatever threat to the relationship may come from within. The failure to be accepting of another may be precisely the failure to accept within oneself the feelings experienced in the relationship.

I believe that there may often be unfortunate consequences when and if this mutuality is not recognized. In seeking to aid a person whose thoughts, feelings, and behavior have become problematic, the offering of acceptance is vital, whether it come from counselor, pastor, or friend. Anyone who offers such a relationship is likely to be appreciated, admired, and perceived as virtuous, strong, or superior. If the relationship then disintegrates, the fault tends to come to rest on the problematic nature of the person in need of help. The last state may be worse than the first.

A more balanced view would not so readily place the blame all on one side. Positive attributes of the helper may be as real a threat to the relationship as any of the negative characteristics of the other. The reputation, competence, and power of the helper provide no basis for absolving the helper from all responsibility if the relationship deteriorates. Necessary and desirable as reputation, competence, and power may be, the threat to the relationship which arises because of them has to be recognized and dealt with as any other threat. Resistance to help cannot be regarded as obtuseness. That puts the responsibility all on one side. It suggests, instead, that the positive attributes of the helper are in some way inhibiting the mutuality of acceptance from which a successful joint enterprise may flow. The superiority of one party over the other, perceived or felt, is a major challenge, a significant threat to creative relationships.

To accept each other is to recognize that differences do exist, and that in the relationship the thoughts, feelings, and actions of one have consequences for the other and vice versa. To accept each other means that we have positive regard for each other in spite of differences which we may experience adversely. With acceptance comes the ability to tell one another what it is that is being experienced, without making the other blameworthy, or responsible, or under pressure to change. It is to forgive, to uphold, and to celebrate the relationship in spite of the offense (threat) whatever its source.

I should explain that I use acceptance and forgiveness interchangeably, following the practice of Paul Tillich and others. In interpersonal relationships there would seem to be no problem with this, implying, though it does, a certain mutuality of responsibility and need. With the understanding of righteousness which has been outlined in previous pages, it seems to me that the same can be said of the dynamic of the human and the divine. Again, mutuality of relationship, or right relationship, comes not through coercion from one side or the other but through a mutual acceptance of the reality of the other in his or her givenness. Right relationship comes about when we accept God as God and creature as creature. As long as God is perceived as wholly other, the creature remains in isolation believing He does the same. But when the reality of God is perceived as the Word made flesh, when Jesus is known as equal to God yet humbles himself and takes the form of a man (Phil. 2:6-8), the alienation is overcome. It is not through any works or pretensions from the human side but through the sacrifice of the other that at-one-ment takes place. Whether between human and human or human and divine, the only basis for mutuality is that of voluntary giving in which rights, privileges, power, claims, and virtues are willingly renounced, though not denied, in the interests of the relationship.

In my thesis I had proposed that "unqualifed acceptance of the person as he is rather than as he may become, and experience by that person that it is so, is a decisive factor in that person's movement toward health. I concluded that acceptance need not be unqualified to be helpful, though lack of acceptance at some critical points may impede the process through the threat to the relationship which is implicit in less than unqualified acceptance." I did not then examine the other side of the coin, the threat to our relationship posed by the patient's willingness and ability to accept me. Her continuing investment in the relationship, and eventually her gracious acceptance of me despite my pushiness bespeaks the reality of her acceptance. Her long delay in confronting me suggests the depth of the threat which my behavior posed and her struggle to accept me with that behavior.

The Relationship of Judgment and Acceptance

Acceptance implies commitment to a relationship and experience by the other that this is so. The ultimate test may be confrontation. Mrs. Jones had experienced my commitment of time, interest, and concern. She had been the recipient of initiatives, information, and opinions from me. I provided her with opportunities to take initiatives with me. In the main, I followed her timetable, making her feelings and views central. I tried to enter into her experience of life. She tested me in matters of religious orthodoxy and encountered differences, but the sense of relationship continued strong. She tested me with her record of moral failure and tortured guilt and found there were some differences between us, but the relationship was not affected. She tested me with expressions of frustration and fear and helplessness, and also with her reversal of direction away from health and toward the prospect of ultimate defeat, but there was no sense of abandonment. Beyond such testing, what further challenge to acceptance remained? She expressed a judgment about me. It came out obliquely at first, indication of the threat involved, then openly. The relationship remained intact because with the judgment she offered forgiveness, even before I confessed my sin and renewed my commitment to be accepting of her, come what may. She demonstrated her own commitment to me, I think, because she had come to trust my commitment to her.

Longterm change is unlikely if it comes solely as the result of an external judgment. Compliance may be attempted, often with little enthusiasm or confidence, often accompanied by resentment. The change may even be durable, but it doesn't necessarily enhance the relationship and may lead to a false sense of security. If change comes about in response to a demand which is perceived to be a threat to the future of the relationship, then the judgment may not achieve anything in the direction of positive change but rather the continuing deterioration of the relationship. Even when the judgment is not primarily external but has inward motivation, the possibilities for positive change are sharply reduced in the absence of a committed relationship. In a committed relationship there is no suspension of judgment but the threat of an end to the relationship is not present. There may be experience of rejection and there may be demand for change, but there is a degree of acceptance which may be the basis for some genuine change. Conditional acceptance is not as powerful as unconditional acceptance and it may not be enough to facilitate the desired change. Judgment and acceptance held together through commitment provide the basis for a new dimension in living and working together.

This is important for the marriage relationship. There is trouble ahead for the person who enters into marriage nurturing the secret hope and intent that the spouse will be changed. On the other hand, the years inevitably bring changes to each partner and those changes have consequences for the other. Judgments, criticisms, complaints, expectations, desires, and dreams all have an inevitable and necessary place. They must receive adequate expression. That is likely only when there is a large measure of acceptance from the other and that, in turn, is likely only in the context of a demonstration that the offended party, actual or potential, is committed to the relationship and that confrontation will not be a serious threat to its continued existence. The sloppy equation of love with permissiveness and the labeling of conflict or criticism as unloving behavior conceals the central feature of love, which is commitment to the relationship.

I have now been married more than thirty-five years and with my wife have raised five children. We have made many decisions and many changes over the years, not without stress or conflict. There was no thought of any weakening of our commitment to each other. Further changes came in me as a result of my clinical pastoral education and my new goals as a chaplain and an educator. My wife also changed in her needs and expectations as the family moved out and her role had to be redefined. So long as our changing was experienced by the other as a demand for change, it was fiercely resisted. The more the commitment was tested and remained in doubt the more resistant and negative our attitudes became.

Happily, the commitment was strong enough that our relationship has survived. We have increasingly been able to relax and to celebrate that acceptance of each other and that commitment and, as a by-product, to hear each other's judgments. Each has changed not in response to demand but in response to the acceptance and the judgments which are possible when threat to our continued relationship is withdrawn.

I can't resist the desire to pursue the analogy and apply it to church relationships. Commitment, it seems to me, is as sorely needed there. I'm thinking of the relationship of pastor and congregation, of pastor and persons, of member and member. Is the church a voluntary society? We tend to function that way. The pastoral relationship is often a fragile one. Members come and go. "It's their business," we say. But is it? Is not membership in the church, symbolized by baptism, a recognition of our belonging, and, when we accept membership as our own, an expression of our commitment to the Body of Christ, to fellow members of his body, and our response to the commitment which God has made to us through Jesus Christ? Our response is voluntary but once our commitment is given should we not proceed as though our relationship is durable, knowing that in such a framework there will be experience of both acceptance and judgment in relation to God and in relation to our peers? Is it not through such commitment that the potential for new growth is to be found, in the freedom of an enduring, caring, loving relationship?

Working in a parish context again, I have had opportunity to see how commitment to persons estranged from me or from the congregation can result in reconciliation. In two instances very irate persons received attention from the ministers and selected members of the congregation. Their hurt was recognized, their anger accepted, their freedom to choose their own course, if need be to break fellowship, was respected, and the care and concern of the congregation was made known. On another occasion it was my frustration and protest which boiled to the surface in a meeting of the church council. When I had vented my feelings for a time and I felt more accepting of the persons who had been the occasion for my outburst, I asked how they felt about the experience. For some it had been traumatic. Ministers aren't supposed to do things like that. For others it was encouragement to be more open with their troublesome feelings and concerns. No one has dropped out. Just about everyone is more attentive to the concerns of those who differ from them. There seems to be more security, more readiness to hear judgments and offer acceptance to each other in spite of disagreement. The relationships of person to person have withstood testing and are the stronger for it, making possible more sharing, more testing, and above all the possibility for change when members are not afraid that their emotions or their concerns will destroy the fellowship. Without judgment there can be no forgiveness. Without forgiveness there is little likelihood of new life.

So the backdrop for the experience of judgment and forgiveness is commitment. Without it judgment cannot be fully heard and there may be no good news in it. That is the significance of Paul's line in Romans, "the wages of sin is death" (Rom. 6:23). With a commitment a relationship exists and there is a basis for hope. A real difficulty appears just here. It is raised over and over again in counseling in one form or another. How can I experience the judgment which I need to hear if I am to grow, and the acceptance which I long for without being sure of the commitment of the other person? If I must have that assurance and if I end up demanding it, does that not threaten the relationship still more? If I can't be sure of the commitment of my spouse, does that mean there is no relationship and therefore no hope? Am I not dependent for my hope on the commitment which isn't there? Only if I insist on seeing it that way. The commitment that is crucial is in my domain. So long as I will a relationship there is one, and for that I have a model.

The doctrine of justification by faith with its judgment and its forgiveness and its promise stands upon the foundation of the covenant which God made with his people. It was his commitment to a continuing relationship. That covenant was understood by many in ancient times to be a bilateral covenant, that is, a two-sided agreement which if broken by one party nullified the obligation of the other. Prophetic voices proclaimed a different understanding beginning with Hosea. Jeremiah talked of a new covenant which, even more clearly than the old, proclaimed that God's relationship with his people could not be ended by their faithlessness, that his commitment and therefore the relationship between God and his people is one which is dependent for its maintenance solely on God, on his nature and his activity. The New Testament (or new covenant) bears that name because of the conviction that in Jesus of Nazareth God acted decisively to restore what had been in jeopardy. Now there is no threat of an end to our relationship with him through our failure, for he is faithful. The man or the woman, the church member or the pastor who is secure in that covenant relationship with God may be able to hear the judgments of an estranged other, to offer acceptance, and to maintain a commitment to that other despite its lack in the other and despite the ambivalence and denial of caring. Such a person may even be able to let the other person go, giving the other freedom in the knowledge that only in freedom is change and growth possible, and still not lose hope. The hope arising from such commitment is not really our doing nor based on our power and faithfulness. Rather it flows from the faith that God has given us in his power and his faithfulness. If he is for us of whom shall we be afraid? (Rom. 8:31).

I was properly humbled some years ago when, as a chaplain, I had some association with a psychiatric patient of Roman Catholic faith. Because she was a Roman Catholic I had kept my relationship with her within strict limits. Not long after her discharge it was reported to me that this woman was singing my praises among her friends and neighbors. Later, she paid a visit to the hospital to see her doctor and took the occasion to seek me out and thank me for helping her. Perhaps it was a false modesty which prompted me to ask her to be my teacher. I asked her to tell me what among the things that I had said or done had proved to be most helpful. I was taken aback when she said she could not identify a single thing. Puzzled, I persisted in my quest. "It wasn't anything you said or did, but when you came onto the ward I saw you and I knew there was hope." She saw in me not my commitment to her but God's commitment to the human race. I was the symbol of the Covenant, in other words, of God's righteousness.

The Universal Need and God's Action

The universality of God's action is implicit in the doctrine of justification by faith. As Paul expounded it, justification applies to everyone who has faith. Faith itself is God's action, "lest any man should boast" (Eph. 2:9).

It is often hard to make that universality real to the sick in mind or to the sinner. Whether clearly identified by such labels or not, there are many people who think or feel that the gospel and the fruits of the gospel are for the virtuous and the strong, not for the weak and the fallen. That was precisely the view of Mrs. Jones, and a continuing dilemma for me was how to convince her that, in truth, it was otherwise. How could I convince her that I was as dependent on the forgiveness of God as she? Telling her so carried no weight. She still differentiated between my status and her own. Later, when she was expressing dissatisfaction with her own achieve- ments in life, I said there were things about myself and my life which I would also like to see changed. She seemed dumbfounded. What could there be about me in need of changing? My achievements to her were so real, my competence and strength so far surpassing her, in her opinion, that she could not identify with me. It is a common phenomenon, the clergyman on a pedestal. It gets in the way of making real the universal need of God's grace. How does it happen and what can be done about it?

The person on the pedestal is in a position like unto that of the righteous man in the Old Testament. (See the discussion of acceptance, page 153). It is assumed by others and sometimes by the individual so perceived that the person who lives an exemplary life is by virtue of that life secure in relationship to God. To perpetuate that perception is to separate persons and to justify the person who suffers by saying that that is the way it is, to be inferior is their lot, there can be no hope of change so they must remain that way, without hope of new life or confidence before God. It is a view which inhibits change. It is self-defeating. It also defies all the efforts of the person on the pedestal to disabuse them of their error.

It is the same dynamic which seems to be operative throughout life, in area after area. In education, in psychotherapy, differences in competence are often perceived as inherent differences in capacity and worth. The overcoming of such resistance to change and personal growth is the subtle challenge confronting teacher, manager, therapist, or friend. "I am different, therefore I can't . . ." is an obstacle not easily overcome. No appeal to reason is likely to exorcise it. No words of wisdom, no pronouncements, no demands, no threats, no exercise of power is likely to remove the defenses and release the potential of a reluctant peer. How can a common humanity be established? How can it become real?

My preoccupation with judgment and acceptance in my study of the interaction between Mrs. Jones and myself did not preclude from my awareness the possibility that even more was involved in that dramatic incident where she confronted me with my nonacceptance of her. By that confrontation my stance was changed and I tended to conclude that it was my change toward accepting her which enabled her to change her direction once more. What may have been equally significant for her was her growing perception of me as a human being like herself, reserved in some measure, as was she, and capable of making mistakes, of wronging other people, as was she. She knew her sins to be many, and she felt chagrin and shame when confronted by them. She had just seen me experience the same kind of distress with the realization that I had not been accepting her as I should. She could offer forgiveness and in that act know that we were on common ground, forgiven sinners. When she identified with me at the point of my weakness, it may have become easier for her to see something of herself in my strength and therein to find a stirring of hope. I know I have felt that way, and I assume that many others have felt the same in respect to Jesus. Recently I had a liberating kind of experience which makes the same point.

I have never known quite what to do with Matthew, chapter twenty-three. For those who need a reminder, it is the chapter which from the begining almost to the end is a series of woes. Woe to you, scribes and Pharisees, hypocrites! It has all the characteristics of a diatribe, and from the lips of Jesus! I am aware, of course, that Jesus stood in the tradition of the prophets and identified himself by his own choice with John the Baptist. None of these men were given to mincing their words! Often in picturesque language they denounced their contemporaries in an effort to awaken them to their peril and urge them to return to the Lord. Why should I not expect and accept the same from Jesus?

Mine may be a very subjective reaction which arises because I am not very comfortable with that part of me with which I have had some difficulty in the past. In my younger days as a minister I was keen and impatient and prone to strong feelings toward those who seemed given to obstruct or oppose my goals. I was inclined to defend such feelings in myself, whether they were expressed or unexpressed, as righteous indignation. The prophetic voice was an honored tradition in which I was pleased to stand. The time came when I was struck with the incongruity of denouncing unloving persons in an angry and uncaring way. Could such angry feelings really be blessed? There was also some

156

problem for me in the fact that there were scriptural admonitions like "Judge not, that you be not judged" (Matt. 7:1) and "Repay no one evil for evil, but take thought for what is noble in the sight of all. If possible, so far as it depends upon you, live peaceably with all" (Rom. 12:17-18). In my experience the expression of righteous indignation in the name of righteous indignation accomplished little that was good and commonly led to further strife.

I know that some critics regard chapter twenty-three as a collection of sayings rather than as one discourse, just as the Sermon on the Mount wasn't delivered in the precise form in which it is known to us. It has even been argued with some force that the editor of the sayings, living and writing long after the time of Jesus, may have incorporated some memories strongly colored by the years of struggle between the young church and the leadership of the Jewish people. That possibility helped me a little at the time I read a book about Jesus written by a modern Jewish scholar who disputed strongly the sweeping denunciations which Matthew especially ascribes to Jesus. Some scribes and Pharisees perhaps deserved it, but there were many like Gamaliel, respected and worthy of respect. My unrest remained.

Then it happened. As part of my present parish-based program of CPE, my students and I keep journals. Three times a week each person writes about events and experiences, feelings and reflections in a journal, then tries to identify scripture passages which might express the same thoughts or feelings, or which address the person in some way. One morning my reflection centered on the meeting of a church committee the night before. I became aware of how strong my negative feelings were toward some of the persons who had been a part of that meeting. When I sought to relate such feelings to scripture I turned to Matthew 23. I read it through. I read it through again. The tone seemed to match my feelings toward those recalcitrant members. Could I be justified in feeling that way? Would it ever be right for me to express such feelings, as Jesus seemed to have done? I wasn't satisfied. All of a sudden it was as if a light had been turned on! How did the chapter end?

"O Jerusalem, Jerusalem, killing the prophets and stoning those who are sent to you! How often would I have gathered your children together as a hen gathers her brood under her wings, and you would not! Behold, your house is forsaken and desolate. For I tell you, you will not see me again, until you say, 'Blessed is he who comes in the name of the Lord.' "

Where is the denunciation? Where is the invective? Only compassion for the city and its inhabitants. Were the scribes and Pharisees excluded? Could it be that Jesus' earlier statements were a combination of prophetic utterances and judgments and ethical precepts of enduring worth coupled with the expression of strong emotions rather than objective and final declarations of truth concerning their fate? Do his harsh words deserve to stand for all time or was their force properly spent the moment they were uttered?

I liked that thought for two reasons. First, it no longer seemed necessary to isolate the scribes and Pharisees, as if God had given up on them. After all, the covenant depends solely on God's faithfulness. Jesus' utterance would then be in the context of a continuing commitment to them. That fits my perception of Jesus in relation to persons, all persons. Second, it seemed to give me a model for dealing with my own feelings. It may be appropriate even to express them in the context of a continuing commitment to those who are the occasion for my distress.

Such an interpretation takes the text of Scripture seriously. I like that. It upholds my perception of Jesus as just and merciful, and I like that. It also helps me to identify with him in his humanity. If I am like him in his exasperation and distress, I find courage to believe that I may become more like him in the strength of his commitment to others, even to those who obstruct and oppose. I need that.

This illustrates for me what the Incarnation is all about.

Differences between Jesus and ourselves are not obliterated. Jesus is still God, and we are still the persons we are. But he is not in splendid isolation on the top of some pedestal. He is not a plaster saint but a person of flesh and blood. Though we are not the same, we have so much in common. God did not impose himself upon us and overwhelm us from his position of power and might. He took his place beside us. Though different, he entered into our human life fully, even to the point of death itself, so that we could appreciate and accept him, not over against us but with us and for us in our struggle to respond to the invitation to freedom and life. That willingness to share the burden, to enter into the struggle, not claiming any superiority of wisdom or virtue, to adopt the role of servant, by one who could do otherwise, is one description of the saving work of Christ.

There are a variety of theories regarding his nature and his work. It is not my purpose to enter into that debate but to mention only one referred to as the kenotic theory. It takes the name from the Greek word "kenosis" which is the keyword in the well-known second chapter of Philippians: "Have this mind among yourselves, which is yours in Jesus Christ, who, though he was in the form of God, did not count equality with God a thing to be grasped, but emptied himself, taking the form of a servant, being born in the likeness of men. And being found in human form he humbled himself and became obedient unto death, even death on a cross" (Phil. 2:5-8). No clinging to a pedestal there! Utter and complete identification with the persons he came to serve. There was no denial of who he was, no renunciation of gifts, no protests of sameness but also no exploitation of others, no abuse of power, no diminuition even of the least among those he met. Kenosis means self-emptying. In this context it meant the setting aside of that which might be a barrier between himself and others in order that they might be raised up. Whatever the merits of the kenotic theory, it seems to me that in this image of the self-emptying Christ we have another model for our efforts.

In order to help others to grow we need not deny the realities of our own life, our gifts, skills, knowledge, moral uprightness, or strength. However, we need not parade them before others, least of all those we seek to help. We can seek to divest ourselves of whatever in us seems to affect our relationships adversely. We can refrain from using the power that we might use over the life of the other. We can concentrate our efforts on discovering what it may mean to take our place alongside the hurting person who cries out for relief. If that seems like denying gifts, it need not be so. As long as there is the clear recognition that in any helping relationship the common denominator is human need, then any gift or skill may have a place. The teacher cannot teach without the student.

Charles Curran, Jesuit priest and teacher at the University of Chicago, has developed an ingenious approach to teaching and learning whereby the student is enlisted to respond to the need of the teacher to teach.[5] With this mutuality of need as the focus, it seems that the resistance to learning is outflanked. The syndrome of the superior dispensing largesse to empty vessels waiting to be filled is supplanted by the active participation of the students in facilitating the efforts of the teacher to meet his or her needs.

There may have been an element of that in my relationship with Mrs. Jones. I was a minister, to be sure, but I was also a student and she could assist me in my learning. Indeed she was and is stimulating my growth right now with her encouragement to work on this book. There is some reason to believe that in so doing she herself is being served.

If this mutuality of need serves student and teacher, counselor and client, pastor and parishioner, it is also true that the judge and the lawyer and the policeman all have needs which cannot be met in isolation. The innocent and the guilty alike have needs which may be served by law enforcement, the courts, and the various services related to them. Reciprocity of need is there, too, not on the basis of sameness but on the basis of a mutuality of need which cannot be satisfied without the other. Until something of that mutuality is recognized and appreciated on the part of each person, the person needing to change, even wanting to change, much more than the person required to change and experiencing difficulty in doing so, will be unduly impressed by or resentful of the achievements and power of the other.

The earnest seeker will turn to the professional because of the reputation established, usually on the basis of preparation and certification. This is as it should be in the church and elsewhere. There is knowledge, and there are skills, abilities, strengths, gifts, and qualities of living acquired and cultivated by professionals, and it is natural that these should be desired by others. How can they be shared, transmitted? Experience suggests that it is not a simple matter of desire on either side. Instruction, direction, and insight are not enough. In all of life, as well as in the Christian life, there is something more required of the seeker and of the would-be benefactor. That something more is real. It is also elusive. There are good teachers and poor teachers and indifferent teachers even as there are outstanding preachers, poor preachers, and indifferent preachers. There are competent therapists and less competent therapists and duds. What is measured in making such judgments is hard to describe. To describe the elusive quality as an art doesn't solve the problem. It simply labels it.

For me that art represents the ability to mobilize the relevant knowledge, skills, and powers to fulfill the professional function in such a way that in the appropriate moment, having identified through encounter the resistances of the seeker to change, the professional offers acceptance of the person at the point of that resistance and divests self of those attributes of competence and strength which normally are a prized possession, to become truly personal about the reality of their common humanity.

That art never develops in a vacuum. It is always in relationship. The nature of the separation between the client and the professional can never be known in advance for it is unique to each individual relationship. The when of the self-emptying, for which Christ is the model, likewise, cannot be known in advance. There is a kairos, a fullness of time, a right moment, but it may be recognized only in retrospect. Hence the how cannot be predetermined. It emerges from the context. It is that which seems right in the moment. In Christian terms it is the prompting of the Spirit.

My experience with Mrs. Jones provides two instances. In two respects she perceived her life to be very different from mine: her sin and her lack of accomplishment. It came very naturally to me to share something of my own vocational setback and uncertainty. It was natural for me to confess my sin with feeling when she confronted me with something I did which I believed to be wrong. When, as part of my confession I shared some of the reasons for the pressure she experienced, attaching importance to my ability to help her change, she must have realized that I was confronted also by my limits, my inability to help her as I wanted to. My limits were as real as hers, and I was not in despair.

How can the professional deal with his own limitations in an authentic way? Is there a denial of weakness? Is there a theoretical admission only of limits? Is there aloofness which defies efforts to becoming known? Is there studied indifference to excellence or blatant display of incompetence? Neither calculated concern for professionalism nor disdain for it will serve. The professional will fall from the pedestal and no one will be helped. If, by contrast, in the context of the effort to help, the professional experiences limits akin to the struggling seeker and can share in a personal way what they are and how they are being faced, there is the possibility that the separation between the strong and the weak may be overcome. The pedestal with its negative connotations will be removed. The strong will be affirmed in their humanity and lose nothing through the laying aside of the claim to power. The weak will be affirmed in their weakness and therein find strength to grow. Paradoxically, the self-emptying of the professional, to whom the seeker has come with faith, will destroy that image and at the same time restore it. In the process the seeker may grasp the truth that weakness and strength, in combination, are part of normal human existence and that as weakness has been experienced so, too, strength will come through.

Faith-At-Work, the interdenominational organization which is seeking to develop a new style of leadership in the churches, notably lay leadership, conducts leadership training workshops which are based on the principle that leadership is not what you do but who you are. Their statement concerning the rationale of their workshops reads, in part:

Hence the stress in the Leadership Training Institutes is not first of all on the teaching or even the improving of what are called leadership skills but on calling forth a quality of being, an authentic life-style. This quality of being is rooted not in talents, roles and skills which our society may reward by a number of payoffs, but in our common humanity and in the uniqueness of our personhood. In order for the training experience based on our common humanity and our individual gifts to work, it must be based on the double motion of the human spirit made possible by the security which comes from faith. The first motion is a stripping away of the security derived from a role or a competence in that role. A person who needs the security of a leadership role in order to function must first die to that role and become an un-leader. He must be crucified and rise again as a human being. The second motion of the spirit is for the leader to become aware of his leadership capabilities as gifts. To see one's leadership ability in this light is to have the freedom sometimes to lead and sometimes to follow and to relate to other people as persons and not as mere objects of leadership. . . . Furthermore to see leadership as a gift is to refuse to absolutize it, to understand that there are no perfect leaders, and to accept failure as a corollary of life and risk.[6]

The same element of paradox surrounds the ultimate human need which arises from the reality of death. We all stand powerless before it. The Christian gospel arises from the faith that Jesus, the Son of God, divested himself of his power and became a human being even to the point of experiencing death and was raised in power. If he shared our life, including the death we must die, then we shall also share his resurrection to newness of life. It is faith in that love and power of God which provides the security to make our self-emptying possible.

The Universal Priesthood of Believers

I am convinced that the saving action of God in Jesus Christ is a paradigm of all helping, healing relationships. The disparity between God and man was, at one and the same time, the occasion for human hope and human despair. In the face of human limitations and helplessness there was need for God's power. In the face of human freedom and fickleness there was the need of God's faithfulness and love. The experience of such otherness, however, did little to overcome the barrier created by their differences. Not until he revealed himself in Jesus Christ did his people appreciate the depth of his love or the value he placed upon them. Not until Christ died and was raised and the Holy Spirit was given did they know the mutuality of the human and the divine as he had made it known. Possessing that faith in him, they received the fruits of his ministry and went forth to minister to others.

The doctrine of justification by faith made central the action of God in Jesus Christ and in the gift of faith to the believer. No intermediary was required. No human agency could effect or guarantee what was available by faith alone. What need, then, for the prayers or the sacramental powers of priests? Yet the understanding and the experience of the Reformers was such that they could not properly free the people of God from dependence on each other. Instead of making each one a priest to self, they proclaimed each person to be a priest to the neighbor, to each other. They believed that in the mutuality of need and in the sharing of gifts born of life's experiences, God's action would be proclaimed, faith given, and power made manifest.

I am convinced that this is true in all helpful relationships within the religious sphere or without. Whether in teaching or preaching, in counseling or psychotherapy, in consulting, organizing, manufacturing, politics, or sales, mutuality of need and concern must be the basis on which people meet or there will be no significant sharing of gifts, no change, no growth, no creativity. In this respect the opportunity and challenge for the religious professional and other professionals—psychiatrists, social workers, psychologists, teachers—is the same. The believing pastor and the believing social worker may start from different points and deal with different subject matter but the dynamics of the helping relationship, where personal change and growth are desired and sought, are, at root, the same. The ability to identify with accuracy the commonality of interest and concern and to receive from each other what each has to offer to the other, that is the essence of the dependence in which we stand as members of the human race. Even the agnostic or the atheist cannot escape the priesthood in that sense.

Sigmund Freud was not a believer in the Christian sense. He was eminently successful as a theorist and a practitioner of the healing art. He discovered that, although the doctor may listen to the patient and may offer interpretations and provoke thought by relevant questions, there is something more involved which has power to release the self and to lead to self-understanding. He described this "something else" in these terms: "The outcome in this struggle is not decided by his [the patient's] intellectual insight . . . it is neither strong enough or free enough to accomplish such a thing, but solely by his relationship to the physician."[7]

Daniel Day Williams, theologian, builds upon this understanding of how help comes to a person. He says that whenever a person seeks help there is actually a search for the real world and for the relation of the self to that reality. This is no mere intellectual quest, and he says the counselor who sees it as such is likely to fail. Feelings are a vital part of the process. But it is not just a matter of feelings between the counselor and the client, important as these may be. Both the counselor and the client stand in a context which is over, against, and between them, a reality in which both of them may find their meaning. As a Christian theologian, Williams offers the interpretation that "the objective reality which stands between persons is God made personal and available to us in Jesus Christ."[8] He warns against understanding this as a pious substitute for the patient exploration of specific problems and emotional patterns of persons by psychiatrists and others. For, as he says:

> Jesus Christ entered fully into our humanity. He took it all, with its endless perplexities and problems upon himself. He offered no simple way out. What he offered was the spirit of love acting in self-identification with human need. Therefore whenever we are honestly probing for reality, with psychological instruments or others, Christ is already present.[9]

What has been discussed primarily as a professional function is really not exclusively professional. This is the age of the volunteer. Many, if not most, professional citadels are being stormed today by the awakened volunteer. Without all the knowledge, mystique, and skills of the professional "many mighty works" are being performed. What do professionals and volunteers have in common? Their personal strengths and weaknesses, and their willingness to share. Years ago Leslie Weatherhead wrote a book about Jesus called *The Transforming Friendship,* but many a testimony could be given regarding the transforming power of human friendship, not of sameness but of mutuality of needs acknowledged and gifts shared.[10] That is ministry, by whatever name.

That which distinguishes Christian ministry from other ministries is the conscious awareness that the service undertaken is made possible through God, made known through Christ, and the conscious commitment along with the service to make known to the receiver the Savior of the world, the source of all wisdom, beauty, and light. In other words, the Christian in ministry is intent upon proclamation of the gospel either by word or by deed.

I earlier raised questions regarding the distinction between professional ministry in the church and the ministry of the laity. Are they ministries essentially different in nature or essentially the same? I argue for the latter. Both flow from the same kind of experience of God as revealed in Jesus Christ. Both seek by word and deed to profess the same faith. The professional has certain advantages in terms of time, the opportunity to acquire knowledge and skills, the opportuity to devote time to others in need. The professional has advantages of role and reputation in a world very conscious of both. But there are disadvantages. Because of his professional role there are myriad demands on his time and attention. Because he is paid for his services, his motivation may be subject to question. Because of his perceived or presumed knowledge and skill there may be the pedestal phenomenon, the more so if his time is also under pressure.

As indicated, this is an obstacle not easily overcome. Just as the professional's spiritual life may be severely taxed in the effort to divest self of very real gifts in the interests of mutuality, so the layperson, from the other side, may be pushed to discover the extent of the gifts which may have been bestowed, as yet unused or undeveloped. For the task both need the grounding of a faith in which to rest secure amidst the risks of the unknown way. What sometimes has to be sacrificed is not too exalted a view but too meek a perception of the self. In fact, some folk, in spite of their professions of faith seem to have so limited a view of their gifts as scarcely to present a self at all. John B. Cobb, Jr., in his book *Theology and Pastoral Care* says that what Christians frequently offer in the name of self-sacrifice is not the sacrifice of a self-transcending spiritual self but the possibility of becoming a self.[11] He says that for many self-assertion may be a necessary step, and that this is justifiable so long as it is affirmed as necessary for the moment and not turned into an ultimate. But Christians, laypersons or otherwise, feeling they have something to offer non-Christians, are bound to face defeat if in their confidence and joy they appear as superior beings. Their profession as laypersons may be as deadly as the professionalism which screens out the personal, the mutuality of human experience, both of gifts and of needs.

How can the professional who is a Christian and the lay believer divest themselves of every vestige of that superiority which, false though it may be, tends to creep in and create a barrier between them and those to whom they seek to minister? I think, though words fail to do justice, that there is more than a hinted solution in my experience with Mrs. Jones. It is not that the doctrine of justification by faith really offers any new theory, any new formula by which to instruct or to manipulate persons in need of repentance or change or growth. It is, however, part of the picture. I upheld judgment for her because I knew it to be operative in my life. I upheld hope for her because I believed there was hope for me. In return, I experienced judgment, acceptance, and hope through her. And each of us knew or came to know that what was happening between us, as we haltingly shared our life together, was not our doing alone but was due to the presence, activity, and power of a third Person. Mysteriously, each in his own way, we were learning what it means to live each day in that faith, "just as I am," offering that self to one another.

Epilogue

In January of 1980, nineteen years after having met Mrs. Jones, I received a short note in which she said she was at last rid of her veteran's pension and would now have to seek employment. There was a note of triumph in her letter as there had been some months earlier when she reported that she was free of medication.

Obviously, whatever had happened between us, the result wasn't of the "lived-happily-ever-after" variety. The beginning was an extended break in the previous pattern of hospitalization. The annual exchange of Christmas letters conveyed without words her continuing struggle to maintain herself outside hospital walls. Ten years later, I learned through a personal visit that there had been three hospitalizations, two of them quite intense, but they were of shorter duration than formerly, and there were increased intervals between them.

My day-long visit in 1972 did not work out as my hostess had planned. Changes were necessary. However, this did not seem in any way upsetting to her. She was neatly and conservatively dressed, living in very plain circumstances. She knew what she wanted me to see in her home city, where we would go for lunch and for dinner. She seemed self-assured in transacting the necessary business and was both courteous and friendly with attendants.

She was obviously pleased to see me. Her memory of my family was accurate, and her recollections of our experiences together much like my own. Without embarrassment, we talked about past symptoms, confessions, and struggles, and subsequent reflections. I was struck with the awareness that she retained many of her former convictions, though with less rigidity. She perceived her confessions to me as real and necessary. She was more accepting of many ideas received through treatment, notably that she had suffered from a psychotic illness since her youth, and the necessity for medication plus psychotherapy. She faulted the pressure of intensive psychotherapy and the permissiveness of doctors regarding sex. She declared that she had opted for the "proper life" and felt better for it.

My taking her guilt seriously, yet accepting her, she considered to be important still. She admitted to experiencing some nonacceptance from me. I noted at the time that "she seemed to find some satisfaction in offering me acceptance in the face of my nonacceptance." When uged to identify what in my counseling with her she found most helpful, she said my contribution was more than time, more than acceptance, that as a man of the cloth I represented the spiritual dimension.

She said that as a result she had come to feel accepted by God, had been able to accept herself including her "wrong impulses" and her own inability to cope with the pressures attending normal living, employment, volunteer work, or anything leading to the necessity of meeting external expectations.

Mrs. Jones reported that she didn't attend church, couldn't cope with the crowds, but that she listened to her pastor on the radio and could speak to him. She spoke of him as "accepting" and contributing to her sense of well-being. Despite her apparent ease in moving about the city, she insisted that apart from two or three friends she didn't socialize very much, relying chiefly on her radio and TV.

When I reported at some length on the importance of my learning with her and the recognition my thesis based upon it had received, she was obviously pleased. When I told her how several professors had urged me to rewrite it for publication, she exclaimed, "Why don't you? It would give me another reason for living."

Of her increased stability in recent years she has said before and since that a black social worker who is also a Christian has been a continuing source of help to her. When I returned home I began work on a manuscript but laid it aside shortly thereafter when I took up new work. Then through circumstances more related to my life than to hers, I lost contact. When I picked up the task again, I realized that although I had exhausted all avenues for tracing Mrs. Jones by mail, I had not tried directory assistance. By this means, I was able to establish contact again before the evening was over.

On my first call, I was informed that Mrs. Jones was out. Calling later I reached her just after her return from a mid-week prayer service! She reported that she now owned her own home, had an older woman companion living with her, and invited my wife and me to stay with her should we ever come that way for a visit.

Signing a consent form for the use of personal material in this book related to her counseling with me, she wrote: "Congratulations! Here's hoping the Faith projected in the book will help some poor mental patient find his way out of darkness."

Notes

Chapter I—The Who and the How of Ministry

1. Thomas J. Mullen, *Renewal of the Ministry* (Abingdon: Nashville, 1963), p. 60.

2. Seward Hiltner, *Ferment in the Ministry* (Abingdon: Nashville, 1969).

3. Report of the Task Force in Ministry, authorized for study in the church by the twenty-seventh General Council of the United Church of Canada, August, 1977, p. 3.

4. Ibid., p. 6.

5. Andre Lemaire, *Ministry in the Church,* trans. C. W. Davies (London: S.P.C.K., 1977).

6. Hans Kung, *Why Priests?* trans. R. C. Collins (Garden City, New York: Doubleday, 1972).

7. Henri Nouwen, *The Wounded Healer* (Garden City, New York: Doubleday, 1972).

8. Henry Nouwen, *Creative Ministry* (Garden City, New York: Doubleday, 1971).

9. Hans Kung, *Why Priests?* p. 50.

10. Ibid., p. 117.

11. Ibid., p. 118.

12. Henri Nouwen, *Creative Ministry,* p. 21.

Chapter III—I Know I'm Helping, but Should I Be Doing More?

1. Harry Stack Sullivan, *The Psychiatric Interview* (New York: W. W. Norton, 1954).

2. Anton Boisen, *Exploration of the Inner World* (New York: Harper & Row, 1962).

3. Victor Frankl, *Man's Search for Meaning* (Boston: Beacon Press, 1963).

Chapter IV—What Has Gone Wrong? Help!

1. Carl Rogers, *Counseling and Psychotherapy* (Boston: Houghton Mifflin, 1942).

Chapter VI— Did the Gospel Help or Hinder?

1. Murray S. Thompson, "The Relevance of the Doctrine of Justification by Faith for Pastoral Care," unpublished thesis, Southern Methodist University, 1964.

2. Quoted in *A Theological Wordbook of the Bible* by Alan Richardson (London: SCM Press, 1950), p. 118.

3. Martin Luther, *Lecture on Romans,* trans. and ed. Wilhelm Pauck (Philadelphia: Westminster Library of Christian Classics, 1961), p. 17.

4. Ibid., p. 18.

5. J. A. Bollier, *The Righteousness of God—A Word Study,* Interpretation VIII, 1954, p. 411.

6. Ibid.

7. John Knox, *The Interpreter's Bible,* "Romans," vol. 9 (Nashville: Abingdon, 1954), p. 393.

8. Karl Barth, *The Epistle to the Romans,* trans. E. Hoskyns (Oxford University Press, 1933), pp. 40-41.

9. John Knox, *The Interpreter's Bible,* p. 428.

10. Anders Nygren, *Commentary on Romans,* trans. C. Rasmassen (Philadelphia: Mullenberg, 1949), p. 180.

11. Hobart Mowrer, *The Crisis in Psychiatry and Religion* (New York: Van Nostrand, 1961).

12. Karl Menninger, *Whatever Became of Sin?* (New York: Hawthorn Books, 1973).

13. Seward Hiltner, *Preface to Pastoral Theology* (Nashville: Abingdon, 1958), p. 20.

14. Daniel Day Williams, *The Minister and the Care of Souls* (New York: Harper & Row, 1961), p. 59.

Chapter VII—My Ministry and Me

1. Edward E. Thornton, *Theology and Pastoral Counseling* (Englewood Cliffs, N.J.: Prentice-Hall, 1964).

2. In Wayne Oates, ed., *Introduction to Pastoral Counseling* (Nashville: Broadman Press, 1959), p. 237.

3. Carl Rogers, *Counseling and Psychotherapy* (Boston: Houghton Mifflin, 1942).

4. Seward Hiltner, *The Christian Shepherd* (Nashville: Abingdon, 1959), p. 30.

5. Charles A. Curran, *Counseling and Psychotherapy* (New York: Sheed & Ward, 1968), p. 295 ff.

6. Unpublished material, "Rationale of Leadership Training Institutes," Faith-At-Work (Canada), Inc., Hamilton, Ontario, 1978.

7. Sigmund Freud, *A General Introduction to Psychoanalysis,* Eng. trans. (New York: Liveright, 1955), p. 387.

8. Daniel Day Williams, *The Minister and the Care of Souls* (New York: Harper & Row, 1961), p. 66.

9. Ibid., p. 70.

10. Leslie Weatherhead, *The Transforming Friendship* (London: Epworth Press, 1928).

11. John B. Cobb, Jr., *Theology and Pastoral Care,* Creative Pastoral Care series (Philadelphia: Fortress Press, 1977).